Y0-BZZ-300

THE NEW IMMIGRANTS

Filipino Americans
Indian Americans
Jamaican Americans
Korean Americans
Mexican Americans
Ukrainian Americans
Vietnamese Americans

Jamaica

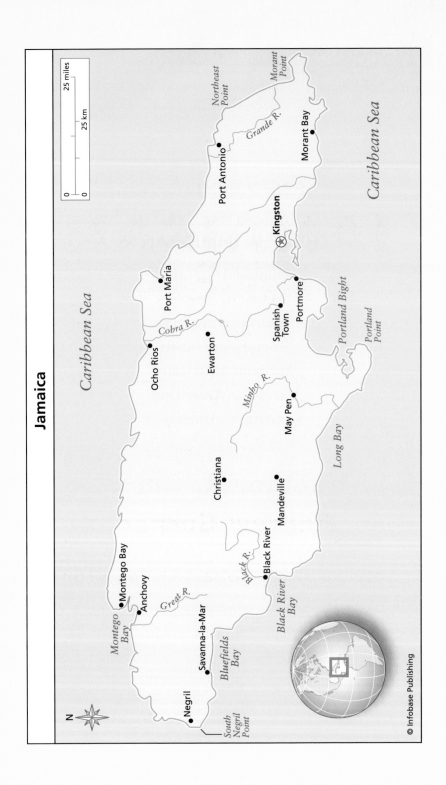

© Infobase Publishing

THE NEW IMMIGRANTS

JAMAICAN
AMERICANS

Heather A. Horst
Andrew Garner

Series Editor: Robert D. Johnston

Associate Professor of History,
University of Illinois at Chicago

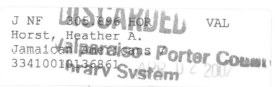

CHELSEA HOUSE
PUBLISHERS
An imprint of Infobase Publishing

Frontis: Jamaica is located due south of Florida and is the third-largest country in the Caribbean. According to the U.S. Census Bureau, there were 736,513 people of Jamaican descent who lived in the United States in 2000.

Jamaican Americans

Chelsea House
An imprint of Infobase Publishing
132 West 31st Street
New York NY 10001

ISBN-10: 0-7910-8790-5
ISBN-13: 978-0-7910-8790-9

Library of Congress Cataloging-in-Publication Data
Horst, Heather A.
  Jamaican Americans / Heather A. Horst and Andrew Garner.
    p. cm. — (The new immigrants)
  Includes bibliographical references and index.
  Summary: Grades 9—12.
  ISBN 0-7910-8790-5 (hardcover)
  1. Jamaican Americans—History—Juvenile literature. 2. Jamaican Americans—Social conditions—Juvenile literature. 3. Immigrants—United States—History—Juvenile literature. 4. Immigrants—United States—Social conditions—Juvenile literature. 5. Jamaica—Emigration and immigration—Juvenile literature. 6. United States—Emigration and immigration—Juvenile literature. I. Garner, Andrew. II. Title. III. Series.
  E184.J27H67 2007
  305.896'97292073—dc22   2006025904

Chelsea House books are available at special discounts when purchased in bulk quantities for businesses, associations, institutions, or sales promotions. Please call our Special Sales Department in New York at (212) 967-8800 or (800) 322-8755.

You can find Chelsea House on the World Wide Web at
http://www.chelseahouse.com

Series design by Erika K. Arroyo
Cover design by Takeshi Takahashi

Printed in the United States of America
Bang EJB 10 9 8 7 6 5 4 3 2 1
This book is printed on acid-free paper.

All links and Web addresses were checked and verified to be correct at the time of publication. Because of the dynamic nature of the Web, some addresses and links may have changed since publication and may no longer be valid.

Contents

Introduction

Robert D. Johnston

At the time of the publication of this series, there are few more pressing political issues in the country than immigration. Hundreds of thousands of immigrants are filling the streets of major U.S. cities to protect immigrant rights. And conflict in Congress has reached a boiling point, with members of the Senate and House fighting over the proper policy toward immigrants who have lived in the United States for years but who entered the country illegally.

Generally, Republicans and Democrats are split down partisan lines in a conflict of this sort. However, in this dispute, some otherwise conservative Republicans are taking a more liberal position on the immigration issue—precisely because of their own immigrant connections. For example, Pete Domenici, the longest-serving senator in the history of the state of New Mexico, recently told his colleagues about one of the most chilling days of his life.

6

In 1943, during World War II, the Federal Bureau of Investigation (FBI) set out to monitor U.S. citizens who had ties with Italy, Germany, and Japan. At the time, Domenici was 10 or 11 years old and living in Albuquerque, with his parents—Alda, the president of the local PTA, and Cherubino, an Italian-born grocer who already had become a U.S. citizen. Alda, who had arrived in the United States with her parents when she was three, thought she had her papers in order, but she found out otherwise when federal agents swept in and whisked her away—leaving young Pete in tears.

It turned out that Alda was an illegal immigrant. She was, however, clearly not a security threat, and the government released her on bond. Alda then quickly prepared the necessary paperwork and became a citizen. More than six decades later, her son decided to tell his influential colleagues Alda's story, because, he says, he wanted them to remember that "the sons and daughters of this century's illegal immigrants could end up in the Senate one day, too."[1]

Given the increasing ease of global travel, immigration is becoming a significant political issue throughout the world. Yet the United States remains in many ways the most receptive country toward immigrants that history has ever seen. The Statue of Liberty is still one of our nation's most important symbols.

A complex look at history, however, reveals that, despite the many success stories, there are many more sobering accounts like that of Pete Domenici. The United States has offered unparalleled opportunities to immigrants from Greece to Cuba, Thailand to Poland. Yet immigrants have consistently also suffered from persistent—and sometimes murderous—discrimination.

This series is designed to inform students of both the achievements and the hardships faced by some of the immigrant groups that have arrived in the United States since Congress passed the Immigration and Naturalization Services Act in 1965. The United States was built on the ingenuity and hard work of its nation's immigrants, and these new immigrants—primarily from Asia and Latin America—have, over the last several decades, added their unique attributes to American culture.

Immigrants from the following countries are featured in THE NEW IMMIGRANTS series: India, Jamaica, Korea, Mexico, the Philippines, Ukraine, and Vietnam. Each book focuses on the present-day life of these ethnic groups—and not just in the United States, but in Canada as well. The books explore their culture, their success in various occupations, the economic hardships they face, and their political struggles. Yet all the authors in the series recognize that we cannot understand any of these groups without also coming to terms with their history— a history that involves not just their time in the United States, but also the lasting legacy of their homelands.

Mexican immigrants, along with their relatives and allies, have been the driving force behind the recent public defense of immigrant rights. Michael Schroeder explains how distinctive the situation of Mexican immigrants is, particularly given the fluid border between the United States and its southern neighbor. Indeed, not only is the border difficult to defend, but some Mexicans (and scholars) see it as an artificial barrier—the result of nineteenth-century imperialist conquest.

Vietnam is perhaps the one country outside of Mexico with the most visible recent connection to the history of the United States. One of the most significant consequences of our tragic war there was a flood of immigrants, most of whom had backed the losing side. Liz Sonneborn demonstrates how the historic conflicts over Communism in the Vietnamese homeland continue to play a role in the United States, more than three decades after the end of the "American" war.

In turn, Filipinos have also been forced out of their native land, but for them economic distress has been the primary cause. Jon Sterngass points out how immigration from the Philippines—as is the case with many Asian countries—reaches back much further in American history than is generally known, with the search for jobs a constant factor.

Koreans who have come to this country also demonstrate just how connected recent immigrants are to their "homelands" while forging a permanent new life in the United States. As Anne Soon Choi reveals, the history of twentieth-century Korea—due to Japanese occupation, division of the country after World War II, and the troubling power of dictators for much of postwar history—has played a crucial role in shaping the culture of Korean Americans.

South Asians are, arguably, the greatest source of change in immigration to the United States since 1965. Padma Rangaswamy, an Indian-American scholar and activist, explores how the recent flow of Indians to this country has brought not only delicious food and colorful clothes, but also great technical expertise, as well as success in areas ranging from business to spelling bees.

Jamaican Americans are often best known for their music, as well as for other distinctive cultural traditions. Heather Horst and Andrew Garner show how these traditions can, in part, be traced to the complex and often bitter political rivalries within Jamaica—conflicts that continue to shape the lives of Jamaican immigrants.

Finally, the story of Ukrainian Americans helps us understand that even "white" immigrants suffered considerable hardship, and even discrimination in this land of opportunity. Still, the story that John Radzilowski portrays is largely one of achievement, particularly with the building of successful ethnic communities.

I would like to conclude by mentioning how proud I am to be the editor of this very important series. When I grew up in small-town Oregon during the 1970s, it was difficult to see that immigrants played much of a role in my "white bread" life. Even worse than that ignorance, however, were the lessons I learned from my relatives. They were unfortunately quite suspicious of all those they defined as "outsiders." Throughout his life, my grandfather believed that the Japanese who immigrated to his rural valley in central Oregon were helping Japan during World War II by collecting scrap from gum wrappers to make weapons. My uncles, who were also fruit growers, were openly hostile toward the Mexican immigrants without whom they could not have harvested their apples and pears.

Fortunately, like so many other Americans, the great waves of immigration since 1965 have taught me to completely rethink my conception of America. I live in Chicago, a block from Devon Avenue, one of the primary magnets of Indian and Pakistani immigrations in this country (Padma Rangaswamy mentions Devon in her fine book in this series on Indian Americans). Conversely, when my family and I lived in Storm Lake, Iowa, in the early 1990s, immigrants from Laos, Mexico, and Somalia were also decisively reshaping the face of that small town. Throughout America, we live in a new country—one not without problems, but one that is incredibly exciting and vibrant. I hope that this series helps you appreciate even more one of the most special qualities of the American heritage.

Note

1. Rachel L. Swarns, "An Immigration Debate Framed by Family Ties," *New York Times*, April 4, 2006.

Robert D. Johnston
Chicago, Illinois
April 2006

1

Exodus

Jamaica is a 4,411-square-mile (11,424-square-kilometer) Caribbean island that lies south of Cuba and west of Hispaniola. A ridge of mountains runs down most of its length. This ridge is high enough in places to produce some of the best coffee in the world. The island's lush tropical climate, beaches, and warm sea attract thousands of tourists, the majority from the United States. It is also a country that about 550,000 people in the United States and 212,000 in Canada have called home.

Jamaica is a country shaped by colonial conquest, slavery, and the sugar trade. Today, its population of 2.6 million is 98 percent Afro-Caribbean, with fewer than 2 percent claiming Indian, European, Chinese, or other ancestry. The ancestors of the majority of Jamaicans were brought to Jamaica from West Africa forcibly, to work as slaves on the sugar plantations.

It is this African heritage, together with the history of their struggle for freedom and independence, that has so marked Jamaican identity.

In order to appreciate the contributions and influence of Jamaican Americans on the North American communities in which they live, we need to understand Jamaican culture and identity. Four things are most important to Jamaicans: food, music, religion, and travel. Although Jamaican culture comprises many other elements as well, these are arguably the most influential when considering Jamaican migration to North America.

FOOD

Jamaica has a large urban population, but the countryside is highly valued. It is a source of "proper" food, such as the fresh mangoes and breadfruit people always bring with them when visiting relatives in the cities and towns. Land ownership and the ability to grow or catch one's own food were rights for which many Jamaicans fought and died for when they were slaves. This symbolic importance may explain why the distinctive foods of Jamaica are carried throughout the world by the expatriate community.

Wherever Jamaicans settle, shops and stores open to supply ingredients for saltfish and ackee, jerk chicken, curried goat, rice and peas, Jamaican patties, spiced bun, and potato pudding. These might be washed down with a can of Red Stripe (a Jamaican beer) or some white rum. Jamaicans visiting family living overseas always bring some distinctively Jamaican food with them and will go to great lengths to prepare the food in the "right way." This often means getting the freshest ingredients possible and cooking outside on an open fire.

MUSIC

For a small country, Jamaica's contribution to world music is immense. Jamaicans boast a greater output of recorded music

Food is Jamaica's second-largest export and an integral part of the island nation's culture. Pictured here is Burchell Rhoden, a chef for Walkerswood Caribbean Foods in Walkers Woods, Jamaica. Rhoden is preparing scotch bonnet peppers, one of the main ingredients in jerk seasoning.

per person in their country than anywhere else in the world. Reggae, and the music of Bob Marley and the Wailers, has had one of the biggest influences on the international music scene. Marley's album *Exodus*, recorded in London in 1977, was voted *Time* magazine's album of the century. Jamaican music has had such an important effect on popular culture in the United States, Canada, and the United Kingdom that it is worth understanding where it comes from.

Jamaica's earliest musical influences were carried from throughout West Africa to the slave plantations. Plantation music was therefore a fusion of forms. "Mento," one type of music with strong African roots in its drumming rhythms, is still played today.

The influence of Christianity, and its hymn singing, was also important to Jamaican culture. Hymns would often be sung to syncopated clapping, which can still be heard in many churches in Jamaica today. Both the rhythms and the religious language learned in church powerfully influenced reggae music, a musical style that most people associate with Jamaica.

At the end of World War II, Jamaicans were listening to the big swing bands popular with American soldiers. These bands would play to large audiences on "lawns" around Kingston. Jamaicans returning from work in the United States brought the sounds of bop and rhythm and blues back home. These new sounds, developed in black communities, were being played in Miami and New Orleans and on radio. With the help of a new phenomenon, the sound system, these sounds were reinterpreted. Rather than pay for a large band, organizers played the recordings to huge numbers of people on the lawns. Several sound systems competed with each other for audiences and were hugely popular. For many people, this was the only way to hear the new sounds.

In the late 1950s and early 1960s, black rhythm and blues became white rock and roll. Meanwhile, in Jamaica, "ska" became the music that best captured the optimism felt by Jamaicans when the country gained its independence in 1962. Ska was fast and upbeat. It also sold well in the United Kingdom. By the early 1970s, a new generation of young people in Jamaican ghettos was looking for work but could not find any. These young adults felt increasingly excluded from the optimism of the post-independence generation. They began to dance in a slower and more menacing way. They developed a group identity and were known as "rude boys"—for them, it was a way of being somebody rather than nobody. The slowed-down beat became "rock steady," then very quickly morphed into reggae.

Conventional democracy did not seem to work for the people in the ghettos, and many kids raised in the ghettos

Created in the late 1960s, reggae can be traced to traditional African Caribbean music, as well as rhythm and blues music from the United States. The distinctively Jamaican music genre earned worldwide recognition through the work of Bob Marley, who is pictured above performing at a concert in Stockholm, Sweden, in 1978.

began to look for alternative belief systems. The new religion of Rastafarianism, combined with ideas about black power, seemed to offer a viable alternative to what was seen as the "corrupt" Western system. Rastafarians also emphasized the importance of Africa to music and to hanging onto cultural roots. The resultant reggae style was social music, commenting on inequalities, protesting oppression, and looking for redemption in Africa.

Meanwhile, the use of sound systems was evolving. Dance patrons liked to hear new versions of songs they already knew, so copies were made of the originals, with portions of the vocals left out (these were called "dub-plates"). Then deejays added their own comments, a practice called "toasting." Toasting drove audiences wild and led directly to the remix cultures used in rap, hip-hop, and dancehall music. Today, artists such as Beenie Man and Bounty Killer expand the dancehall tradition, whereas Sizzla is a new exponent of Rastafarianism. Jamaican music remains as vibrant as ever.

RELIGION

Jamaica is fundamentally a nonsecular society. About 80 percent of the population describes itself as Christian, but there are also Rastafarians, Jews, Muslims, and Hindus. Faith plays a role in almost every aspect of life. Business offices might start the week with a short prayer and Bible study session;

RASTAFARI

The Rastafari faith has its roots in the teachings of black nationalist Marcus Garvey and the Bible. Garvey urged Jamaicans to "look to Africa, where a Black King shall be crowned." In 1930, Ras Tafari Makonnen was crowned king of Ethiopia and became Emperor Haile Selassie, last in a line of kings said to stretch back to King Solomon and Makeda, the Queen of Sheba. Garvey and his followers (called Rastafarians) took this to be proof of Selassie's divinity.

Rastafarians see Haile Selassie's ascension to the throne as the second coming of God (Jah) and Africa as their spiritual home. They believe they are living in Babylon, in the system of Western corruption and "slave mentality." Most follow basic ideas taken from the Bible. They don't cut their hair (Leviticus 21:5) and are very proud of their dreadlocks. They follow a strict "Ital" diet, where all the food is natural and unprocessed. They avoid meat and, quite often, fish (Proverbs 15:17).

Rastafarians also favor "bush medicine," using indigenous plants to heal their sick. They consider most other medicine

radio shows and newspapers have regular slots for pastors to answer questions; and churches run schools, support health-care provision, and provide subsidized housing. In fact, most Jamaicans can, and often do, quote sections of the Bible. Sundays are taken up with church attendance, and services can be daylong affairs. Most Jamaicans living in North America share this religious outlook.

When the first slaves were brought to Jamaica, they carried with them African religious traditions. The planters tried to quash these practices by banning drumming and breaking up meetings. When missionaries began arriving in the late eighteenth century, they were often in strong disagreement with the planters. At heart, this was because they argued that

unnatural. Such practices can include surgery and cutting of the flesh, which they believe is wrong. Homemade "roots wine," made from many local plants, is often drunk and is believed to build up stamina. Ganja (marijuana)—which they call "the herb"—is seen as a religious sacrament and an important part of their meditation "reasonings." Reasoning shows them truth and uncovers the wickedness of the world.

At first, women "sistren" were viewed as impure and a corrupting influence on a man. They needed to be guided by a "King-man" to know the faith as a "Rasta Queen." Since the 1970s, however, women have begun to claim their own independent place within the Rastafari movement. The Rastafarian colors of red, green, gold, and black are represented in houses, clothes, and paintings and are well known internationally through the success of Bob Marley's albums. Red represents the blood spilled in the history of oppression, green represents the fertile land, gold the victory over "Babylon," and black is occasionally used to represent the population of Jamaica.

Jamaicans are adherents of a variety of religions, including Rastafari, which is practiced by approximately 5 to 10 percent of the population. Pictured above is a group of Rastafarians waving their flags at the opening ceremony of the Ras Tafari Global Reasoning conference in July 2003. The colors of the Rastafari flag are an important symbol of the movement: red stands for the blood of martyrs, green stands for the fertile land of Jamaica and Ethiopia, and gold stands for victory over Babylon and the wealth and prosperity of Africa.

slavery was inherently un-Christian. Owners grudgingly allowed slaves to attend church on Sundays. The practice of training promising young men to become deacons to help run the churches allowed a more educated group of black activists who could then use their sermons to start political action. This, combined with concerted religious and political efforts in Britain, eventually led to the emancipation (freeing) of the slaves in 1834.

Many African traditions continued with beliefs in Obeah (evil spiritual power or witchcraft) and forms of belief in a supernatural power that animates the material world. Spirits were thought to have an influence on the living and must be

Religious Groups in Jamaica	
Religious Affiliation*	**Percentage**
Church of God	21.2
Seventh-day Adventist	9.0
Baptist	8.8
Pentecostal	7.6
Anglican	5.5
Roman Catholic	4.0
Methodist	2.7
United Church of Christ	2.7
Jehovah's Witness	1.6
Brethren	1.1
Moravian	1.1
Other, including some spiritual cults	34.7

* Statistics from 1999 Jamaican Census

respected, pacified, and praised through dancing, offerings, and prayer. In the nineteenth century, Jamaicans combined these traditions with a movement sweeping through the Christian church in a series of revivals (1831, 1840, 1860, 1865, and 1883). These popular movements challenged the status quo of colonial structures and of the established churches. Zionism and Pukumina were forms of revivalism that carried African traditions and Christianity into new, unique forms of Jamaican worship. Zionism deals with the heavenly spirits and angels. Pukumina addresses the "ground spirits." Some of the drumming techniques used in revival ceremonies found their way into Rastafarianism and the rhythms of reggae.

The main change in Jamaican religious practices in the twentieth century was the growing number of denominations registered in Jamaica. These grew from 92 in the 1970s, to 169 in the 1980s, to 286 in the 1990s. By 1999, there were 606 denominations, most of which were evangelical churches. These groups tend to be socially conservative (for example, teaching strong role segregation between men and women) and follow the fundamentalist teachings of Bible-Belt America. There is also an overall indication that attendance is becoming more gender specific, as relatively fewer men go to church. Among the younger generation, church attendance may be dropping, but most will still have been inducted into church rituals.

CONCLUSION: TRAVEL AS TRADITION

Together with food, church, and religion, migration (often called "travel" in Jamaica) is an important part of Jamaican life. In a country born of forced migration, travel has always been regarded as a necessary option. Escaped slaves would walk into the interior of Jamaica, where they found they could avoid oppression and work for themselves. As the city of Kingston grew, rural Jamaicans would travel there to seek work and opportunity. In the nineteenth and twentieth centuries, Jamaicans emigrated throughout the Caribbean, Central America, the United Kingdom, and North America on a temporary and permanent basis. For many Jamaicans, migration to North America is simply a part of life and provides a much-needed safety valve for an island where there are fewer opportunities to advance in life than there are overseas.

When they arrive in North America, Jamaicans bring with them a cultural willingness to work, a strong sense of religious duty, and the foods and music that make them unique. This book is about these Jamaicans and their contribution to life in North America.

• Study Questions •

1. Find out something about Jamaican food. What spices are used to flavor the food? Where do the ingredients come from? Can you get them where you live? How much do they cost?

2. What is the contribution of Jamaica to world music?

3. What does the music of Bob Marley talk about?

4. Why is religion important to Jamaicans?

5. Is Jamaican migration to North America new? Where else have Jamaicans emigrated?

2

My Island in the Sun

Jamaica has a unique social and cultural history. This history has a powerful influence on Jamaican identity and can help us understand some of the motivations of Jamaicans living in North America. The people who arrived as slaves constantly struggled against the injustices of an unequal system. Generations of resistance and rebellion eventually won them freedom, then independence. This chapter follows this history of resistance, which strongly influences Jamaicans today.

AMERINDIANS AND THE FIRST EUROPEANS

The Taino people—Arawak-speaking Amerindians—arrived in Jamaica about A.D. 900. They probably traveled up the Caribbean archipelago from South America. They used stone tools, woven baskets, and nets to forage and fish for food and lived in dispersed settlements near a reliable source of freshwater. It is difficult to estimate the Taino population in Jamaica when the first Europeans arrived in the Caribbean, but it could have been as many as a million people. Because of the tropical climate, archaeological records remain scarce.

When Christopher Columbus landed on the northern coast of Jamaica on May 6, 1494 (his second voyage to what he believed was the Far East), the Tainos attacked his party. They had heard about Spanish violence from their neighbors on Hispaniola, today's Haiti and Dominican Republic. The Tainos were easily defeated. Columbus remarked that he had never seen a "fairer isle," called it Santiago, and claimed it for Spain, but he did not stay long. In fact, it was 16 years later in 1510, that a permanent Spanish settlement was established on the North Coast. However, the new settlers had not chosen the site well. It was surrounded by swampy land, and fever began to threaten the settlers. A new capital on the southern coast, known today as Spanish Town, was established in 1534.

For the next 121 years, Jamaica served primarily as a stopping-off point between Spain and the riches of her other colonies. Ships would arrive, pick up fresh food supplies, and be cleaned and repaired. During this period, bananas, sugarcane, horses, and cattle were introduced on the small farms the settlers started. The Spanish also managed, through a mixture of deliberate cruelty and accidental infection, to wipe out virtually the whole Taino population. Like most Amerindians, Tainos had little resistance to European diseases and died in the thousands. It is thought that a few survived and joined forces with runaway slaves, but by all accounts the deaths amount to genocide.

THE BRITISH CONQUEST AND BEGINNINGS OF RESISTANCE

The Spanish colony in Jamaica was not well protected, and Spanish Town was attacked twice by the British—once in

1596, then again in 1643. In 1655, armed forces sent by Oliver Cromwell, Britain's Lord Protector, landed in Jamaica and quickly established control of the country. The Spanish were finally driven out of Jamaica in 1660, but not before they freed and armed their slaves, who joined the growing band of Maroons. The Maroons were a community of escaped slaves who, from the safety of Jamaica's hilly and inaccessible interior, resisted colonial power and the ravages of a slave society. Many of the original Maroons were from modern-day Ghana in West Africa and of Coromantee descent. In their communities in Cockpit Country and the Blue Mountains, the Maroons effectively created free societies that are celebrated today in Jamaica as part of a long resistance to slavery and desire for independence.

To secure their hold on Jamaica, the British began to fortify what is now Kingston Harbor with forts, particularly at Port Royal. They encouraged "buccaneers"—pirates—to make Port Royal their base for attacks on Spanish ships and bases. It was thought that by officially sanctioning these individuals as privateers, the new colony would be protected and it would also get 10 percent of the haul. Port Royal became a boom town and gained a swashbuckling reputation that was one inspiration for the film *The Pirates of the Caribbean*. When an earthquake plunged most of Port Royal into the sea, many commentators of the time saw this as evidence of punishment for the vices practiced there. In 1670, a treaty with Spain that officially recognized British rule in Jamaica marked the end of the heyday for the buccaneers. However, pirates such as Henry Morgan and Calico Jack Rackham continued to operate well into the eighteenth century.

More important and far-reaching changes were happening in the country's economy, however. Settlers found it difficult to compete with Virginia in growing tobacco, so they turned to sugar production. As the taste for sugar in Europe

LEONARD PARKINSON, a Captain of MAROONS,

taken from the Life.

Before the Spanish were driven from Jamaica by the British in 1660, they freed and armed their slaves. Some of these former slaves, known as Maroons, created free societies in the Jamaica backcountry. Maroon captain Leonard Parkinson is depicted in this 1796 engraving, which originally appeared in *The Proceedings of the Governor and Assembly of Jamaica in regard to the Maroon Negroes.*

increased, Jamaica became the world's biggest producer of sugar. Consequently, the owners of the sugar estates, called "planters," became incredibly wealthy. Along with this wealth came political power and the ability to protect the sugar trade. Most owners were absentee landlords, who delegated responsibility to overseers in Jamaica, while they spent their money and protected their interests in Britain. This trade was built on the appalling misery and inhumanity of slavery. The Spanish had brought African slaves to Jamaica, but the amount of labor needed to grow sugarcane caused a dramatic increase in the slave trade.

SLAVERY

When the sugar industry took off, slavery was already a well-established practice that provided labor throughout the Americas. The Atlantic slave trade in the 1700s was dominated by British merchants and followed a triangular trading route. Trinkets and other goods were bartered in West Africa for slaves. This human cargo was then tightly packed in unspeakable conditions for the "middle passage" between Africa and the Caribbean. Those who survived illness, starvation, and the brutality of the traders were then sold at auction, and the ships returned to Britain full of sugar, rum, and spices. In the early days, many Africans sold to the merchants had been captured in war. As demand increased, chieftains on the coast organized raiding parties to capture more prisoners. Between 1751 and 1790, 80 percent of the slaves delivered to Jamaica were from three areas: the Akan-Ashanti people from Ghana; the Yoruba, Ibo, and Ibibio from Nigeria; and some groups from Central Africa.

The slave trade was organized in such a way as to break the bounds of family, kin, language, and culture by selling family members to different owners. By mixing slaves from different areas, the plantation owners ensured that English became the main language for communication. Some scholars have argued that the middle passage served as a fundamental discontinuity, forcing a complete rupture with the cultures of Africa. Indeed, treatment on the sugar estates was often equally brutal, where living conditions were squalid, and torture and painful death were used to discourage rebellion. Evidence exists that, despite this brutality, many Africans found ways to preserve aspects of their identity in language, in dance and music, in food—and in rebellion.

Slave revolts in Jamaica were more numerous and on a larger scale than anywhere else in the British West Indies or the United States. They occurred, on average, every five years during the eighteenth century and were invariably brutally crushed. Part of the reason for the high number of rebellions, despite the appalling punishments doled out to those captured, was the high ratio of slaves to whites in Jamaica. Another reason was the proximity of mountains, in which it was relatively easy to hide. Perhaps the most important reason, though, was the desire for freedom. This desire also found intellectual expression in the social and religious ideas prevalent at the beginning of the 1800s. These included the abolitionists making the case against slavery and challenging the power of the planters to dominate politics in Britain, and missionaries who challenged the complacency of the established church.

For example, the Christmas Rebellion in 1831 was led by Sam Sharpe, a slave in Montego Bay and a leader in the Native Baptist Church. The slaves were well aware of the campaign for the abolition of slavery in Britain. They also knew the planters were bitterly opposed to ending slavery; there was a rumor that slavery had actually been abolished but that the planters were simply not going to tell anyone. At first, Sam Sharpe organized a campaign of passive resistance, in an attempt to force the planters into declaring the end of slavery. This campaign rapidly became a full-blown revolt. It lasted for just 10 days but involved nearly 20,000 slaves and most of the western part of Jamaica. In the end, Sam Sharpe and 500 slaves were either killed or executed, but the rebellion served to intensify the abolition debate and provided yet another powerful moral case for justice.

THE ABOLITION OF SLAVERY

The abolition of slavery was a hotly debated topic in Britain at the turn of the nineteenth century. Although popular pressure for abolition was clear, the planters in the British West Indies mounted fierce opposition. In Jamaica, the planters even toyed with the idea of seceding from Britain. The planters' influence began to dissipate as the taxes levied on their business competitors were gradually reduced and the sugar beet proved effective competition in the European market. In fact, the British Parliament prohibited the trading of slaves in 1807, but the actual abolition of slavery and the emancipation of the slaves did not happen until 1834. Even then, they were not given unconditional freedom but were expected to work, unpaid, for a further six years under an "apprenticeship" scheme. This was finally abandoned in 1838, and the former slaves were able to demand wages or to take their labor elsewhere. Not surprisingly, many chose to set up small farms rather than continue to work at the sugar estates.

Faced with an acute shortage of workers, and unwilling to pay proper wages, the planters looked to other methods of securing cheap labor. Indentured labor, a practice whereby people were given a passage from their home country and brought to Jamaica in return for a number of years of work on the estates, was seen as the answer. Small numbers of workers had already been brought from Germany, China, and the Middle East, but the largest group of indentured laborers came from India—35,000 between 1845 and 1917. In reality, conditions were little better than they were under slavery. The workers found it impossible to save money, as their pay was regularly docked to "pay" for food and other items they needed.

THE ROCKY ROAD TO INDEPENDENCE

Between 1850 and 1930, despite a steadily evolving economy, a series of economic downturns and food shortages highlighted the continuing inequalities between the white minority and the Afro-Jamaican majority. The introduction of free trade in sugar ended the protection Jamaican sugar producers had enjoyed, and by the end of the nineteenth century, only a few sugar estates remained active. To fill the economic void, bananas, coffee, and citrus fruits were introduced as cash crops. During the American Civil War of 1861 to 1865, a naval blockade cut off crucial supplies to Jamaica, which caused food shortages.

Against this background of economic insecurity, two issues served to highlight the continuing need for change. First, there was the issue of land. Unless they could find somewhere to farm, black Jamaicans had little choice but to return to the sugar estates. Planters were well aware of this fact, and they made it as difficult as possible for black Jamaicans to own land. They raised rents and threw "squatters" off unused land. Today, land "capture" is viewed as a legitimate means of establishing ownership of unused land by many Jamaicans. The second issue concerned justice. The planters still dominated the magistrates' courts and imposed draconian penalties for minor violations that were often the result of poverty.

Things came to a head in Morant Bay in 1865. The authorities removed two people from the parish council: a magistrate who was seen as too impartial and George William Gordon, a mixed-race businessman. Gordon was one of the few non-whites who had managed to get elected despite property and wealth rules, which favored the landowners, and he was openly sympathetic to the plight of poor black Jamaicans. On October 11, a group of people led by Paul Bogle attacked the police station. They took weapons and released prisoners, and killed 18 soldiers and council members.

The incident was followed by minor rebellions in outlying plantations and, fearing that the unrest would spread, the governor ordered a clampdown. About 437 people, including Paul Bogle and George Gordon, were killed or executed, and thousands more were flogged. Because the suppression of the Morant Bay Rebellion horrified people in Jamaica and Britain, the Jamaican Assembly was abolished and direct rule was established from Britain. Although this move undermined self-government, it did allow reforms to be passed that the planters would have blocked.

During the end of the nineteenth century, the banana and tourism industry began to thrive. In fact, early tourism (from the 1890s) used the banana boats that plied up the East Coast of the United States to bring tourists back to Port Antonio, foretelling of the growth of a major modern industry for Jamaica. The benefits brought by new industries withered in the face of the Great Depression that took hold of the United States in the 1930s. There were riots in Kingston, and strikes were common. In one strike at the Frome sugar factory in 1938, clashes between police and workers left several people dead and caused protests throughout the island. The leader of the strike, Alexander Bustamante, founded the first trade union in the Caribbean, and his cousin Norman Manley, a lawyer, founded the People's National Party (PNP). Both fed the fires of nationalism that had been lit by Marcus Garvey during the 1920s.

At the end of World War II, a new constitution introduced universal adult suffrage, and elections were held. Bustamante split from Manley and the PNP to form his own party, the Jamaica Labor Party (JLP), and won the next two elections. It was Manley and the PNP who tackled the issue of independence when they won in 1955. The PNP worked toward establishing a West Indies Federation linking Trinidad, Tobago, and Jamaica. The federal model was soundly rejected by the electorate in 1961. On August 6, 1962, Jamaica became an independent state

Norman Manley (left) and his cousin Alexander Bustamante (right) were anticolonial advocates who supported universal suffrage for Jamaica's citizens. Manley founded the left-wing People's National Party (PNP) and went on to serve as premier of Jamaica from 1959 to 1962; while Bustamante served as the country's first prime minister from 1962 to 1967.

within the British Commonwealth, with the JLP in power and Bustamante as prime minister.

GARRISON POLITICS

The JLP stayed in power until the 1972 elections. By then, the differences between the two parties were wide. The JLP preferred a procapitalist economic program and favored the United States. Michael Manley (the son of Norman Manley) and the socialist PNP rejected closer ties with the United States and instead looked for better terms by trading with other developing countries in the Southern Hemisphere.

With his election victory in 1972, Manley promoted an agenda of "power to the people," with policies such as literacy campaigns, land redistribution, minimum wage, public housing, and used increased business taxation to pay for it all. His policies deliberately set out to change the balance of economic and political power that had until then rested predominantly with white and mixed-race Jamaicans.

Politics became increasingly polarized in the lead-up to the 1976 elections. Edward Seaga, then leader of the JLP, attacked the "Communist" PNP administration. More disturbing was the increase in political violence, particularly in Kingston. In the ghettos of Kingston, the political parties had turned areas into "garrisons," arming their supporters and encouraging intimidation to recruit voters and drive away opposition. It did not take long for these garrisons to become strongholds for vigilante-style "big men" engaged in gang-based criminal activities.

Manley declared a state of emergency and introduced severe antigun laws, but the damage had been done. Lack of capital and foreign investment, empty shelves, and drastic cuts in social programs alienated many Jamaicans. The 1980 elections were violent, with hundreds killed in shootouts and open gang warfare. The people turned to Seaga and the JLP for hope, and he immediately reestablished Jamaica's relationship with its largest neighbor, the United States.

JAMAICA TODAY

The polarized politics of the 1970s and 1980s have ended. When the PNP was reelected in 1989, there was no return to anti-American and antiwhite rhetoric. Many Jamaicans are disillusioned with politics; they lament political corruption, as the party in power dispenses favors to its supporters. Crime is also

During the 1976 Jamaican parliamentary election, Prime Minister Michael Manley declared a state of emergency to protect voters from armed political parties. Pictured above are two trucks—one filled with policemen, the other with soldiers—traveling through the streets of Kingston just prior to the election in December 1976.

a major concern. The garrison communities remain a safe haven for gangsters, the drug trade brings billions of dollars to drug barons, and countries such as the United States and Great Britain return convicted Jamaicans, who are then free as soon as they arrive home.

On the other hand, the Jamaican economy has become far more stable. Tourism, agriculture, and bauxite remain the mainstays of the Jamaican economy, whereas the substantial remittances (money sent back to Jamaica from family working overseas) help to ease the debt owed by the government to foreign banks. Jamaica was where the first all-inclusive resort was established, and this sector of the tourism market continues to grow, as large, new hotels are built every year. Finally, as we

USING POETRY TO DESCRIBE EVERYDAY LIFE IN JAMAICA

Louise Bennett-Coverley (1919–2006), better known as "Miss Lou," was one of Jamaica's most loved cultural icons. A comedienne, poet, actress, performer, and activist, Miss Lou charmed the hearts and minds of Jamaicans and African Americans worldwide through her spirited poems and performances.

Using Jamaican dialect (a combination of standard English and nonstandard African-derived languages called patois), Miss Lou wrote witty poems about the everyday lives of Jamaican men and women. Her work lifted the stigma of talking "Jamaican." Dressed in traditional Jamaican plaid skirt and headscarf, Miss Lou gave performances that brought figures such as Anancy (a spider and popular character in Jamaican stories), and songs such as ring-ding singing games, and practices such as "labrish" (chitchat) to the fore of Jamaican social and cultural life. One of her most famous poems, entitled "Colonization in Reverse," speaks of the irony of Jamaicans migrating to England after years of being colonized by Britain.

In her later years, Louise Bennett-Coverley traveled the world, where she promoted and lectured on Jamaican music and folklore. She settled in the Toronto, Canada, area, where she received an honorary degree from York University. On Jamaican Independence Day (August 6) 2001, she also received one of Jamaica's highest honors, the Order of Merit (OM), for her years of service to her island home. Bennett-Coverley died in July 2006.

shall see in other chapters, Jamaican exports, particularly music and sports, play a larger role on the international stage than might be expected of such a small island.

Louise Bennett-Coverley (1919–2006) was one of Jamaica's most loved cultural icons. Known affectionately as "Miss Lou," she received worldwide acclaim for her contributions to the arts and culture.

(continues on next page)

(continued from previous page)

"COLONIZATION IN REVERSE"

Wat a joyful news, miss Mattie,
I feel like me heart gwine burs
Jamaica people colonizin
Englan in Reverse

By de hundred, by de tousan
From country and from town,
By de ship-load, by de plane load
Jamica is Englan boun.

Dem a pour out a Jamaica,
Everybody future plan
Is fe get a big-time job
An settle in de mother lan.

What an islan! What a people!
Man an woman, old an young
Jus a pack dem bag an baggage
An turn history upside dung!

Some people doan like travel,
But fe show dem loyalty
Dem all a open up cheap-fare-
To-England agency.

An week by week dem shippin off
Dem countryman like fire,
Fe immigrate an populate
De seat a de Empire.

Oonoo see how life is funny,
Oonoo see da turnabout?
jamaica live fe box bread
Out a English people mout'.

For wen dem ketch a Englan,
An start play dem different role,
Some will settle down to work
An some will settle fe de dole.

Jane says de dole is not too bad
Because dey payin she
Two pounds a week fe seek a job
dat suit her dignity.

me say Jane will never fine work
At de rate how she dah look,
For all day she stay popn Aunt Fan couch
An read love-story book.

Wat a devilment a Englan!
Dem face war an brave de worse,
But me wonderin how dem gwine stan
Colonizin in reverse.

• Study Questions •

I. What role did sugar play in creating modern Jamaica?

(continues on next page)

(continued from previous page)

2. How has Africa influenced Jamaican identity today?

3. Many of the leaders of rebellion against slavery and injustice are celebrated today as national heroes in Jamaica. Choose one hero and describe what he/she did. What did his/her sacrifice achieve?

4. What has independence meant for Jamaica? Describe three positive and three negative results of independence.

5. What role has Miss Lou played in Jamaican life? Why is she such an important figure?

3

Buffalo Soldiers

The number of Jamaicans in North America before 1965 was influenced at first by relations between Britain and her colonies and later by economic factors. Many Jamaicans went to find work in North America, particularly from the 1880s, because lack of work at home made opportunities overseas attractive. These later immigrants to North America began a pattern of Jamaican migration to surrounding countries and along colonial links that continues today. With Jamaicans facing population growth, the periodic collapse of the sugar and banana industries, and limited alternative opportunities at home, immigration always appeared to be a reasonable option.

Many Jamaican immigrants to North America worked in domestic service and as laborers on the railways and in agriculture. A few overcame the limitations of racism to become leaders of their communities and make important contributions to social and cultural development. The first Jamaicans to arrive in North America were the Maroons, a group of freedom fighters who had been transported from Jamaica by the British governor, Lord Balcarres, in 1796.

THE JAMAICAN MAROONS

The following passage describes the power enjoyed by the Jamaican Maroons:

> At last a day came [in 1739] when a company of white soldiers, while toiling up a steep ravine, were obliged to stop from sheer exhaustion. A moment later they heard the click of many gun locks on the mountainside above, and knowing that they had fallen into an ambush, they begged for a parley. The negro leader, a humpbacked fellow of extraordinary ability, named Cudjoe, gave a favorable reply. Then a score or more of machetes began hacking where the gunlocks had been heard, and in a few minutes a great breadth of brush fell like a curtain from the mountainside, revealing a band of Maroons, standing with guns ready to fire on the helpless whites. It was a scene the man-hunters never forgot.
>
> Peace followed this encounter. The treaty gave the Maroons "a perfect state of freedom and liberty," with "full pardon" for attacks on people and property. It gave them 1,500 acres of land on which to settle, and freedom to hunt for game in the mountains. Cudjoe was confirmed in his office as chief, with power to punish crimes that did not deserve death. In return for these immunities and privileges, the Maroons agreed to serve as woods policemen for the capture of runaway slaves.[1]

The treaty agreed by Cudjoe, leader of the Maroons, in 1739 enabled relations between the Maroon communities and the Jamaican government to remain on good terms for 56

In 1739, the British government and the Maroons signed
a treaty of peace that gave the Maroons rights as free men.
However, as part of the terms of the treaty, the Maroons
agreed not to fight against the British and to help capture
runaway slaves and put down slave revolts.

years, despite various slave revolts in the 1760s. In July 1795,
an incident that involved the flogging of two Maroon youths
for killing a tame hog led to the second Maroon war. The
Maroons were incensed because the magistrates sentenced

and punished the men when, under the terms of the treaty, they should have carried out the sentencing. The governor, the Earl of Balcarres, saw an opportunity to make a name for himself. Although the local magistrates urged conciliation, the Earl lied to the British secretary of state for war, saying that there was open rebellion and that he had despatched troops against the perpetrators.

The troops were initially successful and occupied the main Maroon settlements, but by December 1795, the Maroons had not been defeated and received an offer of a treaty of peace. The terms of the treaty were that the Maroons would beg His Majesty's pardon, meet to settle whatever land was going to be given to them, and return all runaway slaves. In return, General Walpole promised that they would not be sent off the island. "My Lord," the general wrote to Earl Balcarres, "it was through my means alone that the Maroons were induced to surrender, from reliance which they had on my word . . . from conviction impressed upon them by me that the white people would never break their faith." Balcarres, however, broke faith with the Maroons and transported them to Nova Scotia. General Walpole resigned his commission in protest.

A group of 543 Maroons landed in North America at Halifax, Nova Scotia, on July 22, 1796, aboard three small transport ships, the *Dover*, the *Mary*, and the *Ann*. The governor of Nova Scotia, Sir John Wentworth, and Prince Edward, duke of Kent, commander-in-chief of the province's forces, welcomed the Maroons. They were impressed by their record of resistance and their demeanor. When the duke of Kent offered them work building new fortifications on Halifax's Citadel Hill, the Maroons accepted the offer and volunteered to work without pay. The duke ordered that they should be paid at the regular rate of nine pence a day, "besides provisions, lodging and clothing."

The Maroons quickly finished building the "Maroon Bastion" to reinforce the new province's defenses. They also formed a militia unit in which two of their leaders, Montagne and John, were made colonels, and two others, Bailey and Jarret, were made majors. The people of Halifax were at first delighted with the added protection and prosperity that the Maroons provided. They had both combat experience and their pay to spend in the community. Soon, there was trouble, however. The Maroons' independent spirit nurtured during a century and a half of guerrilla warfare seemed arrogant to the white citizens, and there were several attempts to have the newcomers expelled. In turn, the Maroons found the climate harsh—several died during the exceptionally cold weather in 1796–97—the food horrible, and the increasing tension with their neighbors difficult to bear. In 1797, they asked to be sent to a warmer climate, but it was not until August 1800 that the government sent them to Sierra Leone aboard the ship *Asia*.

At most a small handful of Maroons stayed on in Canada and integrated with the Free Loyalist Blacks, who later formed part of the community of Africville. The Free Loyalists were slaves who had been promised freedom by the British and who had fled to Nova Scotia at the end of the American Revolution.

WORKING IN NORTH AMERICA

Between 1840 and 1900, the price of Jamaican sugar dropped almost 80 percent. The number of sugar estates on the island fell from 670 in 1836 to just 74 by 1910, drastically reducing the number of workers employed in the industry. Though banana cultivation expanded rapidly,[2] it could never make up for the shortfall created by the collapse of the sugar economy. Following the plummet of sugar prices, thousands of West Indians migrated to the United Kingdom, Cuba, and several Central American and South American countries to find work. The growing influence of the United States in what was increasingly viewed as their "backwater" created more and more economic opportunities for potential migrants. (The weakening of Spanish rule had allowed the United States to occupy Cuba and Puerto Rico.)

The first wave of Jamaican immigrants to North America occurred between 1890 and 1920. At first, many came as seasonal workers, but more and more stayed on permanently. The population of foreign-born blacks grew from 20,000 in 1900 to almost 74,000 in 1920.[3] Between 1904 and 1914, an estimated 44,000 Jamaicans migrated to the United States. Many came to work in the sugarcane fields in south Florida, but, after 1905, New York took over as the main destination of Jamaican emigrants. One reason was that the United Fruit Company began to run banana ships between Jamaica and United States, which enabled many to take advantage of inexpensive tickets. The wave of immigrants in the early twentieth century were also more literate and skilled than the European immigrants who entered the country at the same time, and they were often more literate than the native-born population. It has been estimated that, by the 1930s, a third of New York's black professionals, including doctors, dentists, and lawyers, came from the ranks of Caribbean migrants.

The U.S. Immigration Act of 1924 drastically stemmed the tide of Caribbean immigration to the United States. The numbers plummeted from 10,630 in 1924 to only 321 in 1925. The act was aimed at restricting nonwhite and southern and eastern European immigration. Between the two World Wars, opportunities for migrants decreased, and a wave of immigrants returned to Jamaica. Immigration only picked up again at the start of World War II. Buoyed by an expanding war economy, thousands of Caribbean immigrants were brought in to alleviate severe labor shortages in the United States, Canada, and Britain. In the United States, many Jamaicans again went to work in agriculture, particularly in Florida's sugar estates. By the end of the war, they lived throughout the United States.

THE STRUGGLE FOR EQUALITY

A remarkable member of the early Jamaican-Canadian community was Robert Sutherland, who lived in Ontario. Sutherland was born in Jamaica in 1830. He became the first black lawyer and the first known university graduate of African descent in Canada. To put this into perspective, he started at Queen's University in Ontario in 1849 at a time when slavery was still practiced in the American South. Sutherland excelled at Queen's and graduated in 1852 with an honors degree in classics and mathematics. He then studied law at Osgood Hall and was called to the Ontario Bar (became a lawyer) in 1855. Sutherland settled in Walkerton, Ontario, and practiced law until his death in 1878 at age 48. He left his entire fortune, about $12,000, to the university. As this was a significant sum in those days, his bequeath made him Queen's first major benefactor.

Despite his remarkable success and generosity, Sutherland soon faded from the consciousness of Queen's institutional memory. Not until the 1980s, when a group of student activists rediscovered Sutherland's Story and began to agitate for the university to recognize his contributions, did this situation change. In 1997, The Robert Sutherland Visitorship was established with a prize. The Visitorship enables the university to invite a speaker who has expertise in the areas of equity, community diversity, and race relations to Queen's each year. The Robert Sutherland Prize is presented annually "to a graduating and self-defined student of colour who has shown leadership and initiative at Queen's, most specifically in the area of encouraging and fostering diversity on campus."

Unfortunately, stories like that of Robert Sutherland are remarkable precisely because it was often so difficult for black people to overcome the prejudices of the other communities in America. During the early and mid-1900s, many Jamaicans who had arrived for educational opportunities became involved in the struggle for racial equality. For example, in Harlem, which

(continues on page 50)

MARCUS GARVEY AND THE UNIVERSAL NEGRO IMPROVEMENT ASSOCIATION (UNIA)

Marcus Mosiah Garvey was a crusader for black nationalism and a founder of the Universal Negro Improvement Association (UNIA). Garvey was born in St. Ann's Bay, Jamaica, in 1887. He was the youngest of 11 children, 9 of whom died in childhood.

Garvey left school at 14 to learn the trade of printing, but soon started to travel abroad. He witnessed the suffering of black workers caused by poor working conditions and racial discrimination. When Garvey returned to Jamaica from London in 1914, he established the UNIA to promote black solidarity and pride. The UNIA found opposition in many of the lighter-skinned middle-class Jamaicans, however, who did not want to be identified as blacks.

In 1916, at age 28, Garvey immigrated to Harlem. The following year, he established a branch of the UNIA in New York City. By 1920, there were 1,100 branches in more than 40 countries. He taught that blacks would be respected only when they were economically strong, and he encouraged the establishment of black-owned businesses. Garvey set up the Black Star Line, which had four ships plying between the Caribbean and the Americas, along with publishing houses, grocers, restaurants, and laundries.

Garvey also taught that Africa was the black ancestral home and that it should be taken back from European domination. He pledged to develop the infrastructure of the black-governed nation of Liberia in 1920. In the same year, the UNIA adopted the Declaration of the Rights of the Negro Peoples of the World. This document detailed injustices and condemned discrimination. It also protested against the practice in the education system whereby black children were taught white superiority.

In 1925, Garvey was charged with mail fraud while selling stock in the failed Black Star Line enterprise. He was imprisoned and, on his release in 1927, was deported to Jamaica. He was welcomed there by a large crowd. In 1929, Garvey founded the People's Political Party (PPP). In 1935, he left Jamaica for London and worked there until his death in 1940.

Marcus Mosiah Garvey was born in St. Ann's Bay, Jamaica, in 1887. In 1914, he founded the Universal Negro Improvement Association (UNIA) and he later helped organize the first American black nationalist movement while he lived in Harlem.

CLAUDE McKAY AND THE HARLEM RENAISSANCE

Claude McKay was the youngest of 11 children born to a peasant farmer and his wife in Jamaica. He published his first two books of poetry, written in patois, before he was 21. McKay emigrated from Jamaica to the United States in 1912, where he was shocked by the intense racism he encountered.

McKay is considered to be one of the most important writers of the Harlem Renaissance, the literary and creative flowering of black consciousness. His book of poems, *Harlem Shadows*, published in 1922, served as a precursor to this movement because

Born in the village of Sunny Ville, Jamaica, in 1890, Claude McKay became one of the most influential figures of the Harlem Renaissance. The author and poet was an advocate of civil liberties and racial solidarity, and his book *Home to Harlem*, which was published in 1928, is believed to have been the most widely read novel by an African American up to that point.

in it McKay introduced an angry and defiant attitude toward racial prejudice in America. McKay condemned his experiences living as a black man in America and embodied his feelings in the best known of his poems, "If We Must Die," and in several others (see "America," "The White City," and "The Lynching").

McKay was also able to convey respect, sympathy, and compassion for the lives of the African-American underclass about which he wrote (see "Spring in New Hampshire," "The Harlem Dancer," "The Tired Worker," and the title poem, "Harlem Shadows"). McKay's poetry espoused his political beliefs but also explored the broad range of human life. McKay traveled in Europe for 12 years following the publication of *Harlem Shadows*. Although he continued to publish (*Banana Bottom* appeared in 1933), he was dogged by poverty and ill health. McKay became an American citizen in 1940, and he never returned to Jamaica.

"THE LYNCHING"

HIS Spirit in smoke ascended to high heaven.
His father, by the cruelest way of pain,
Had bidden him to his bosom once again;
The awful sin remained still unforgiven.
All night a bright and solitary star
(Perchance the one that ever guided him,
Yet gave him up at last to Fate's wild whim)
Hung pitifully o'er the swinging char.
Day dawned, and soon the mixed crowds came to view
The ghastly body swaying in the sun
The women thronged to look, but never a one
Showed sorrow in her eyes of steely blue;
And little lads, lynchers that were to be,
Danced round the dreadful thing in fiendish glee.

---

* *The Poems of Claude McKay* is available online at *http://www.theotherpages.org/poems/mckay00.html.*

(continued from page 45)

already had the largest Caribbean population outside of Kingston, Jamaica, a movement had begun to take shape. The area experienced an explosion of artistic, cultural, and social forms of writing that became known as the Harlem Renaissance. After generations of repression, African Americans began to rethink their place in America, to claim a unique identity, and to fight inequalities based on skin color. Jamaican writers such as Claude McKay were at the forefront of this social and cultural revolution. At the same time, African Americans were finding their political voice. Marcus Garvey, another Jamaican, established the Universal Negro Improvement Association (UNIA), which campaigned for black rights and recognition.

• Study Questions •

1. What factors led to the Maroons arriving in Halifax, Nova Scotia?

2. How have political realities influenced the numbers of Jamaican immigrants to North America?

3. Why was Marcus Garvey's message so popular among the black populations worldwide?

4. What role did the Harlem Renaissance play in challenging racial prejudice?

4

Jamaica Farewell

In the world, where territories are divided into political units, what we call nation-states, the ability of people to move or migrate from one country to another is determined by the laws and rules of the countries. Governments make decisions about who can move where based on their ideas about what their country is about and what they want their country to look like in the future. Migrants also weigh their choices about where they want to move based on the situation in which they were born and now live, as well as the potential opportunities that await them in countries such as Canada and the United States. This chapter compares the major policy changes in the United States and Canada after 1960. It discusses how changes in immigration laws gave Jamaicans the chance to move to North America. These laws also determined how long they could stay and what kinds of jobs they could do.

MIGRATION TO THE UNITED STATES

As we discussed in previous chapters, Jamaicans have migrated to North America since the turn of the twentieth century to find seasonal work on farms, to attend college, and to help with nursing shortages in the United States and Canada. In the United States, Jamaicans worked at the United Fruit Company and on the Florida sugarcane farms, but this type of migration nearly stopped when the McCarran-Walter Act was passed in 1952, because the act restricted the immigration of Caribbean peoples from British territories.

Steady migration started again after the government passed the Immigration and Naturalization Services Act of 1965, which

With the passage of the Immigration and Naturalization Services Act of 1965, many Jamaicans have been able to travel to the United States on work visas. Pictured here are Jamaican workers gathering peppers on the Sam Mazza farm in Colchester, Vermont.

changed the ways that the United States decided to admit people into the country. Between 1924 and 1965, the largest number of immigrants to the United States came from the United Kingdom, Ireland, and Germany. Instead of focusing on a person's citizenship, the 1965 act grouped countries into regions (the Eastern and Western hemispheres), which made it easier to provide visas for immigrants based on labor shortages and the need to reunite family members who had been separated.

Focusing on a potential immigrant's region of origin rather than nationality effectively opened the doors to the "new migration" of Asians, Africans, Latin Americans, and Caribbean islanders. In 1968, the U.S. government passed an amendment to the Immigration and Naturalization Services Act of 1965 that based the number of immigrants who received visas more on the skill levels of immigrants and the need to fill jobs in special occupations. In addition, a quota system was developed; at this time, the Caribbean[4] as a region received a yearly entrance quota of 120,000.[5]

In 1976, an additional amendment limited immigrant visas for all countries in the Eastern and Western hemispheres to 20,000 annually, although spouses, children, and other dependents admitted under the family reunification were not counted within the annual limitations. For the Davis family, the change in policy in the 1960s opened up new opportunities. Mr. Davis, who worked in the construction industry, decided to try his luck in Miami, Florida, in 1986, leaving his wife and only son in rural Jamaica. In the early years, he would travel to Florida every year, earn a little money, and come back home. He used the money he earned to pay for his wife's education at a teacher's college.

In 1990, after making a few friends and business contacts, Mr. Davis decided he wanted to apply for a visa to live in the United States permanently. By this time, his wife was a teacher at a local high school and he had three young sons to support. They decided that he would travel to the United States alone and then, eventually, apply for his family to join him. Mrs.

Davis, on the other hand, decided that she wanted to keep the boys in school in Jamaica because she felt their education would be better, and a few years later the couple had saved enough money to buy a house. Each summer, one of the boys would travel to Fort Lauderdale to visit their dad, and he came home at Christmas. As Peter, his oldest son, finished high school, he decided to join his dad in Florida, where he could work and attend community college.

In the 1990s, the 1965 immigration act that allowed Mr. Davis to receive a visa was modified once again: It increased the number of people who could enter the United States to 700,000 each year. In addition, the Immigration and Naturalization Service (INS) started a "Diversity Lottery" to encourage immigration from underrepresented countries. Applicants who met the criteria for entry were randomly selected by a computer program. Because the number of Jamaicans entering the United States over a five-year period is more than 50,000, Jamaica is not considered an underrepresented country.

After the September 11, 2001, terrorist attacks, the U.S. Congress passed the Uniting and Strengthening America by Providing Appropriate Tools Required to Intercept and Obstruct Terrorism Act of 2001 (United States PATRIOT Act). The legislation, aimed at defining and preventing terrorism and securing the nation's borders, encouraged a series of immigration reforms. In 2002, measures such as biometric technologies (for example, electronic fingerprints), as well as machine-readable and tamper-proof passports were installed in order to better monitor the movement of immigrants into and out of the United States.

MIGRATION TO CANADA

Jamaicans migrated to Canada in small numbers throughout the early 1900s. As in the United States, the increase of Jamaicans coming to Canada was caused, in part, by the British government. Parliament passed the Commonwealth Immigrants Act in 1962 and a White Paper in 1965, and both pieces of legislation made it more difficult for Jamaicans and other Commonwealth citizens to enter the United Kingdom. After World War II, Jamaica's status as a colony and member in the Commonwealth made it easier for Jamaicans to move to the United Kingdom.[6] Between 1956 and 1960 alone, 11.2 percent of Jamaica's total population boarded boats for the United Kingdom. From 1955 to 1968, 191,330 Jamaicans arrived in Britain. It was the single largest group of migrants from Jamaica during the twentieth century. Most Jamaican migrants were semiskilled and unskilled, and they worked predominantly as hospital personnel and nurses or in transportation for companies such as British Rail.[7]

With the virtual closure of the United Kingdom to Jamaicans and other Commonwealth citizens in the 1960s, Jamaicans began to look for other places to move. They focused mainly on Canada and the United States. In 1962, the Canadian government passed the Immigration Regulations, which attempted to end racial bias in immigration policy. The new law allowed potential immigrants to apply for visas either independently or as dependents (family members), without considering their national origin. The move away from race and ethnicity as the most important factor in deciding if a person could receive a visa was furthered with the Immigration Act of 1967. This act attempted to make the receipt of visas more equitable by introducing a point system that ranked potential immigrants in terms of their education, age, job prospects, language skills, and economic resources.

The effect of the Immigration Act of 1967 was dramatic. Before 1967, most immigrants were from Europe; by the mid-1970s, the majority were from Asia, Latin America, Africa, and the Caribbean. In 1976, a new immigration act that strengthened the 1967 Immigration Act's interest in unifying families was passed. This new act also separated applications from immigrants from applications from refugees (people who apply to enter Canada because they are being harassed or persecuted in their own country). It also attempted to stop discrimination against immigrants on the basis of race, national or ethnic origin, color, religion, or gender.

In 2002, another immigration law, the Immigrant and Refugee Protection Act, went into effect in Canada. This act, passed after the September 11, 2001, attacks on the United States, had three goals: (1) to work toward increasing the success of family reunification as well as refugee protection; (2) to update the point system and the ways that professional and skilled workers receive visas; and (3) to more closely identify immigrants. Since 2003, immigrants have been required to register and carry a Permanent Resident Card, a procedure designed to more efficiently monitor Canadian immigrants.

OTHER IMMIGRATION PROGRAMS

Temporary Work Programs

With the move away from farming communities and the increase in large-scale farms beginning in the mid-twentieth century, the United States and Canada experienced labor shortages in a number of industries. In response to this shortage, special temporary work programs were created. In 1966, Canada began its Seasonal Agricultural Worker Program (SAWP), which allowed foreign workers to come to Canada to help during planting and harvesting periods, when qualified Canadian workers were not available.

In the United States, the Immigration and Nationality Act of 1952 established the H-2 visa, which allowed individuals to immigrate temporarily to find seasonal jobs. The jobs were created to allow individuals from developing countries such as Jamaica to come to the United States for up to a year (but not more than three years) in order to work in hospitality programs in hotels or in the farming industry.

Organizations such as the Ministry of Labor in Jamaica help recruit farmworkers. For those with temporary contract visas, air fares are paid and housing is provided for up to six months.

In addition to working on American farms, many Jamaicans use the H-2 visa to work in the hospitality industry. Pictured above is Henry Bernard of Montego Bay, Jamaica. A waiter at Coonamessett Inn in Falmouth, Massachusetts, Bernard was one of 84 Jamaican workers who worked for the inn during the summer of 2005.

For example, Winston is a 40-year-old man who participates in Canada's Seasonal Agricultural Workers Program. He describes his migration over the last 16 years:

> When I go for the 6 months I get paid every week ... we do pruning, picking fruit [peaches, apples] in Canada, Ontario. I live on the farm in a farm house and I don't have to pay any rent and I am responsible for my own food. It [the pay] depends on how much hours like $10 CA [Canadian] a hour, every week $200 CA per week ... and I try to save like three-quarters of it or so.... They [the company] pays it [airfare] when we go, but when we return they draw it from our pay.[8]

Individuals like Winston find some benefits to this seasonal migration. (There were about 11,000 seasonal workers in Canada from the Caribbean and Mexico in 1999.) It allows them to work hard for six months and then spend three or four months in Jamaica living off the money earned while they scrimped and saved in Canada. Yet, others argue that these programs do not go far enough. For example, Stephanie Black's documentary entitled *H-2* tells the story of men working sugarcane plantations in Belle Glade, Florida, where they perform hard and dangerous work while earning less than minimum wage. These migrant workers also have little opportunity to relax or go outside the plantation, and they are not allowed time to learn other job skills. They can also be deported, or sent back to their own countries, without question. In addition, although wives, husbands, or children can come with the worker while he/she is on the H-2 and seasonal agricultural visas, the cost of bringing a family is often too high, because other family members cannot work in the United States or Canada.

DIFFERENCES BETWEEN U.S. AND CANADIAN POLICIES

Immigration policies in the United States and Canada differ in many ways, such as the Canadian use of the "points" system and the United States' attention to quotas. Despite these differences, both countries opened their borders to non-European immigrants in the 1960s and have considered the importance of diversity and multiculturalism. Moreover, throughout the 1990s and 2000s, each country restated the need for family reunification and made this one of the most important reasons to give permanent residence visas to Jamaicans. Consequently, in the United States, Jamaicans have formed large communities in cities such as New York and Miami. In addition, Jamaica consistently remains one of the top 10 "sending countries" in terms of immigration statistics.

Jamaicans in Canada represent a much smaller percentage of the overall immigrant community (and the Jamaican diaspora at large) than they do in the United States. Their numbers have tripled between 1995 and 2004, which suggests that the emphasis of the Immigrant and Refugee Protection Act of 2002 on family reunification may also change the Jamaican-Canadian community in provinces such as Ontario.

CONCLUSIONS

Throughout this chapter, we discussed the immigration policies in the United States and Canada. Since the 1960s, the political climate called for the liberalization of immigration. The loosening of immigration controls allowed Jamaicans to migrate to North America in greater numbers. It is often argued that there are more Jamaicans living outside of Jamaica than

Permanent Resident Flow from Jamaica to the United States, 1996–2005*	
Year	**Number**
1996	19,084
1997	17,833
1998	15,123
1999	15,322
2000	15,949
2001	15,322
2002	14,835
2003	13,347
2004	14,430
2005	18,346

Source: U.S. Department of Homeland Security Web site.
  *Available online at *http://www.uscis.gov/graphics/shared/statistics/yearbook/2005/table03.xls*

Permanent Resident Flow from Jamaica to Canada, 1995–2004*

Year	Number
1995	723
1996	1,231
1997	1,720
1998	1,392
1999	1,723
2000	1,658
2001	1,939
2002	1,918
2003	1,737
2004	2,242

Source: Citizenship and Immigration Canada
*Available online at *http://www.cic.gc.ca/english/pub/facts2004/permanent/15.html*

on the island itself. Although sharing similarities, the differing policies of the United States and Canada have shaped the size and proportion of the Jamaican community in each country. In the following chapter, we focus more specifically on the size and other features of Jamaican immigrant population in the United States and Canada.

• Study Questions •

1. What was the main aim of the Immigration and Naturalization Services Act of 1965 in the United States?

2. What was the aim of the Immigration Act of 1967 in Canada?

3. Discuss two ways that the immigration policies of the United States and Canada differed.

4. How did the changes in immigration policies change U.S. and Canadian society?

5. How have the attacks of September 11, 2001, affected immigration policies in the United States and Canada? What has changed?

6. Why did Canada and the United States institute temporary visas for farm- and hotel workers?

7. How has the 2002 Immigrant and Refugee Protection Act affected the Jamaican community?

5

Jamaicans in the Babylon System

In the last chapter, we looked at how immigration policies directly affected the numbers of Jamaicans arriving in Canada and the United States. Now we look at how these policies shaped the Jamaican communities that began to take root in their new countries. Tracing these patterns in large numbers of people is usually called *demographics*. The most important thing to remember is that large patterns always represent real people—individuals who have taken the risk to start their life again in a completely new country. This chapter looks at the Jamaican communities, first in Canada and then in the United States.

MIGRATION TRENDS

Since the 1970s, Jamaica has consistently been counted among the top 10 countries in sending citizens to North America. Only in the last few years has that position changed, as immigration

Since the 1970s, Jamaica has ranked among the top countries in sending immigrants to the United States—in 2003, 13,384 Jamaicans immigrated to the United States. Jamaican Clive Chamberlain is pictured here at a swearing-in ceremony in 2000 during which he became a U.S. citizen.

from Asian countries has increased substantially. From the mid-1960s, immigration laws in both Canada and the United States stopped supporting racial discrimination and moved toward placing greater emphasis on the skills immigrants possessed and how they matched shortages in the labor market. Both countries also began to support the reunion of immigrants with close family members. As a result of these new immigration policies, the kinds of people that emigrated from Jamaica changed.

As we discussed in Chapter 4, one important change was that Jamaicans arriving in North America were better qualified for the job market they found there. Since the 1980s, migration to North America from Jamaica has been dominated by the highly skilled. From 1978 to 1981 alone, 746 professionals, administrative, technical, and managerial staff left Jamaica for Canada.[9] At one point, the "brain drain", or the emigration of Jamaica's most skilled and educated from that country, was high enough to become a matter of public concern in Jamaica, as it still is today. In the end, people's fears were not realized, despite worries about the occasional shortage of qualified workers in hospitals and government departments.

The following news excerpt about the "brain drain" is from a Jamaican newspaper:

> Both the World Bank and the International Monetary Fund (IMF) have recently released studies indicating that Caribbean countries are among the hardest hit by what has come to be called the "brain drain," the migration of skilled professionals.
>
> The World Bank estimate for Jamaica is 80 per cent of university graduates, which ranks us with Haiti. . . . The outward migration of highly trained skilled professionals is a complex issue which may be too simplistically described as a "brain drain," which suggests a purely negative loss. . . .
>
> The less-examined other side of the coin is that developing countries with weak economic growth have never been able to absorb into productive work all of their trained nationals. And many other factors besides education are vital to make development happen. Political systems and governance, economic models, levels of corruption, security issues, and so on, must be factored into the development equation. Migration has been a massive safety valve in these conditions of weak growth and development. And as both the IMF and World Bank studies have acknowledged, remittances from migrants are a valuable source of foreign exchange . . . and help to reduce poverty.[10]

A second result of attempts to match immigrants to skill shortages was that far more women arrived in North America from Jamaica than men. For this reason, women were often the primary wage earners when their families came to join them. Another effect of the demand for certain kinds of skills was that most Jamaicans settled in urban areas. A handful of large cities, among them Toronto, New York, and Miami, host almost the entire Jamaican immigrant community.

JAMAICAN COMMUNITIES IN CANADA

In a 1981 study, when asked their reasons for immigrating to Canada, the majority of those sampled, including Jamaicans and West Indians, responded that it was to "seek adventure." Behind this reason lie a number of other factors that have influenced the Jamaican community in Canada.

In the past, in Canada, immigrants have overwhelmingly come from Europe. Since 1996, this has changed: The majority of immigrants now come from Asia and the Middle East. Jamaica has been an important sending country since the beginning of the twentieth century, and there are Jamaican communities in most Canadian cities, with the largest, nearly 90,000 people, living in Toronto. Even so, this is only 4.9 percent of the residents who were born outside Canada (see table on page 66).

If we go back to the beginning of the twentieth century, between 1900 and 1925, businesspeople could bring in domestics, blacksmiths, and foundry workers from Jamaica if they paid a $15 landing tax. By 1920, there were enough Jamaicans to arrive in Canada for the Reverend Cecil Stewart to establish the Afro-Community Church, the largest black church in Toronto.

In 1955, Canada set up the first regularized program for the admission of Jamaican immigrants. An annual quota of

Top 10 Places of Birth for Immigrants in Toronto, 1996*		
Country	**Number**	**Percentage**
1. United Kingdom	158,070	8.9
2. Italy	146,515	8.3
3. Hong Kong	110,990	6.3
4. India	99,930	5.6
5. China	87,615	4.9
6. Jamaica	**86,910**	**4.9**
7. Portugal	82,105	4.6
8. Philippines	80,860	4.6
9. Poland	74,220	4.2
10. Guyana	60,705	3.4
Total	**987,920**	**55.7**

*Statistics from Multicultural Canada. Available online at http://www.multiculturalcanada.ca/mcc/index.htm.

unmarried females could enter the country on temporary employment visas and obtain permanent residence after a year of domestic service. More than 1,000 women were admitted over a nine-year period. At the same time, Jamaican nurses began to be admitted as "cases of exceptional merit." So many nurses arrived during the 1980s that they formed the Health Care Team in Toronto and the Association of Black Nurses in Montreal.

In 1962, when Canadian immigration policy began to emphasize education skills and job prospects, the numbers of Jamaican immigrants rose from 2,662 in the first half of the decade to 13,439 in the second half—a fivefold increase. Initially, young men were the first to migrate, but by 1969, the balance had swung in favor of females. During the 1970s, more women than men arrived in Canada from

Jamaica, and the immigrants included a higher proportion of children (50–58 percent each year). Of the 62,591 immigrants admitted that decade, 56 percent were women. Also during the 1970s, between 10,000 and 15,000 Jamaican immigrants and their offspring, holding British passports by virtue of birth, migrated from the United Kingdom to Canada. Although Canada needed clerical workers at this time, another factor was at play in luring Jamaicans in this profession to Canada: Professionals in Jamaica were finding life increasingly difficult under the leadership of the People's National Party (PNP), and many families opted to immigrate to Canada as a unit.

In the 1980s, the annual numbers of immigrants fell by nearly half, to 34,124. The pattern of more women immigrating than men continued, but a new trend began to have an impact on Canadian life. Many immigrants had left behind dependants, including spouses, children, and grandparents, who would follow when they could. So, in the 1980s, 43 percent of new immigrants from Jamaica were less than 19 years old. In the 1990s, the growing proportion of young people, particularly between the ages of 10 and 19, increased the number of Jamaican-born and predominantly black children in Canadian schools. Only in the last decade has the number of young people begun to drop off to about 25 percent of Jamaican immigrants.

One factor closely linked to the numbers of young people arriving in Canada is the values and aspirations of their parents. Education has often been the motivation for migration to Canada. Recent studies show that Jamaican migrants have furthered their education on arrival in Canada and hoped for better schooling for their children. Jamaican-born parents are disappointed if their children are not doing well in school or are not trying to improve on the educational or professional attainments they themselves achieved.

The Urbanization of Jamaican Immigrants in Canada		
Province	City	Percentage of Jamaicans in Province Who Live in Cities
Ontario	Toronto	83%
Alberta	Calgary and Edmonton	97%
Manitoba	Winnipeg	97%
British Columbia	Vancouver and Victoria	83%
The Maritimes	Halifax	100%
Newfoundland	St John's	100%
Quebec	Montreal	97%

Jamaicans have shown strong preference for Canadian urban settings, which provide the greatest scope for utilization of their linguistic and occupational skills. Nearly 95 percent live in English-speaking Canada, with 83 percent choosing to live in the province of Ontario. Although Toronto has the largest Jamaican population (and 83 percent of those who live in Ontario), scores of well-to-do families, members of the corporate and legal elites, choose Vancouver. In fact, the number of Jamaicans living outside Canadian cities are so few as to be negligible.

Compared to the first mass migration of Jamaicans to the United Kingdom at the end of World War II, Jamaican immigrants to Canada after 1965 were better educated and occupied higher class and professional positions. There were more females than males, and a significant percentage were under 19. Jamaicans have become well integrated into the multicultural life of many Canadian cities. They usually maintain links to Jamaica even if the second and third generations see themselves as Canadians first.

JAMAICAN COMMUNITIES IN THE UNITED STATES

Overall, more Jamaicans have immigrated to the United States than to Canada. According to the U.S. Census Bureau, there were 736,513 people of Jamaican descent in the United States in 2000, which is 0.3 percent of the total population. Since the 1970s, Jamaica has been counted consistently among the top 10 sending countries until very recently, when it slipped down to eleventh place (see table below).

Many factors that influenced Jamaican immigration to Canada also influenced immigration to the United States. The number of Jamaican immigrants was low until changes in the immigration laws to match immigrants to the work available dramatically transformed the social landscape of the United States. Even though Jamaicans are found in every state, most

Top Sending Countries to the United States (2003)*	
Country	**Number**
1. Mexico	115,864
2. India	50,372
3. Philippines	45,397
4. China	40,659
5. El Salvador	28,296
6. Dominican Republic	26,205
7. Vietnam	22,133
8. Colombia	14,777
9. Guatemala	14,415
10. Russia	13,951
11. Jamaica	**13,384**

*2003 Yearbook of Immigration Statistics.
Available online at http://www.uscis.gov/graphics/shared/aboutus/statistics/IMM03yrbk/2003IMMtext.pdf

Dorothy Johnson did very well as a student in her small village school, to which she walked every day from her house on the other side of a lush, narrow valley. She did so well, in fact, that she landed her first job in the village post office, one of the few roles thought suitable for an educated woman in the 1950s.

One day, a man came into the post office and told Dorothy how beautiful she was. He said she would do well to go to Canada with him. Dorothy's family was worried and asked more. The man recruited Jamaican women to work in Canada. For a deposit, he said, he would help organize the paperwork. He promised a job and a safe place to stay. Dorothy's family decided to take the risk, and everyone contributed toward the deposit and Dorothy's travel ticket.

When Dorothy arrived in Toronto at age 18, however, she found she was sharing a dirty house with many other Jamaican girls. Each had to find her own work and then pay half of what she earned to the man. Work was easy to find, and Dorothy started by cleaning houses and then looking after babies for Canadian families. She regularly sent money home, and in just over a year, she had paid off her debt to the man.

Dorothy then decided to become a nurse, and she worked her way through college. Canada was short of qualified nurses at that time, so when Dorothy finished college, she quickly

stay in major urban centers, such as New York, Miami, Boston, Los Angeles, Chicago, and the San Francisco Bay area. Regionally, most Jamaicans live in the Northeast (59 percent) or the South (30 percent). There are far fewer in the Midwest (4.8 percent) and the West (5.6 percent).

By far, the largest concentration of Jamaican immigrants is in New York, totaling 288,282 in 2003. Estimates that take into account the fact that Jamaicans are often suspicious of official data gathering and that include illegal immigrants are much

found a permanent job and was rapidly promoted. By this time, Dorothy's boyfriend had come over from Jamaica and was working in a garage, parking cars. Soon they were married and started a family.

Nearly a decade later, one of Dorothy's friends told her about the shortage of nurses in the United States. Hospitals in New York were even advertising in Canada. The salaries were much better there, so Dorothy and her husband moved to New York, leaving all but the youngest child with relatives in Toronto. For a while, Dorothy worked in a special ward for new babies, and her husband found work driving limousines. Dorothy's quick wit and efficient work made her very popular with the families coming into the hospital. Eventually, Dorothy realized she could make more money on her own, so she and a friend set up a business providing specialized child care for new mothers in their own home. The nurses would spend four weeks living with a family until the mother felt confident in her new role. They charged a lot for this service but always had to turn people away. Seven years later, nearing retirement, Dorothy and her husband decided to return to Jamaica. They visit North America several times a year to see family and friends. All their children have stayed in America, however—a new, different generation of Jamaican Americans.

higher. About 80 percent of Jamaican immigrants are in permanent work situations, and more than a third of those work in educational services, health care, and social assistance (34 percent). Jamaicans live mostly in central Brooklyn and parts of Queens and the Bronx. At one time, this area of the United States had the densest Jamaican population, but, according to the last U.S. census report in 2000, the county of Broward in the Miami–Fort Lauderdale area now boasts the fastest growing immigrant population of Jamaicans. Jamaicans have arrived here in greater numbers since the 1990s. It is not surprising that Jamaicans refer to Miami and Brooklyn colloquially as "Kingston 22" and "Little Jamaica," respectively.

Where Jamaicans decide to live in the United States is influenced by family connections, the help of friends or church members, job availability, access to college and university education, and weather conditions. However, the biggest influences once immigrants are living and working in the United States are their experiences of ethnicity (being Jamaican), race (being categorized as black), class, and gender. Ethnicity and race are discussed in Chapter 8.

We have already considered how Canadian immigration law encouraged female migration. The same factors affected immigration to the United States. In fact, twice as many young and single females than males left Jamaica for service and factory work in the United States throughout the 1960s. The experience of migration, and especially the increased control of their own money and time, augmented women's sense of independence. This often meant leaving children behind—something that will be discussed in Chapter 7.

In terms of class, the first thing many Jamaicans learn in the United States is that "race" is considered more important. It comes as a shock to many Jamaicans that their neutral observation of a person's skin color at home—where class (what you earn or do) is more important—is translated into a simple distinction between white and black in the United States. The racial identity given to them by American society intrudes on their efforts to define themselves by economic success. To many African Americans, Jamaicans appear to be trying to accommodate to the "rules of white Americans," making African Americans look bad. The tension between these different value systems often make the lives of second- and third-generation Jamaican Americans a series of difficult choices (see Chapter 8). Nearly 60 percent of Jamaicans work in management, professional roles, and office and sales occupations.

Employed Civilian Population 16 Years and Older		
Occupation	**Number**	**Percentage**
Management, professional, and related occupations	43,646,731	33.6
Sales and office occupations	34,621,390	26.7
Production, transportation, and service occupations	19,276,947	14.9
Material moving occupations	18,968,496	14.6
Construction, extraction, and maintenance occupations	12,256,138	9.4
Farming, fishing, and forestry occupations	951,810	0.7
Totals	**129,721,512**	**100**

The median income for Jamaican households in 1999 was $40,276, just below the national median income of $41,994. Looking at the Jamaican household income table on the next page, it is possible to see that 42 percent of households earn $50,000 or more—a good indicator of middle-class status.

CONCLUSION

In both Canada and the United States, Jamaicans over-whelmingly live in cities, where they can take advantage of job opportunities. Immigration policies encouraged skilled Jamaicans, particularly women, to move to North America. In the United States, more than a third of Jamaican newcomers are managers or professionals and about 45 percent work either in education, health or social services, or manufacturing and retail trade. Canadian-Jamaican enclaves tend to be much

Jamaican Household Income Table (1999)

Income	Number	Percentage
Less than $10,000	10,067,027	9.5
$10,000 to $14,999	6,657,228	6.3
$15,000 to $24,999	13,536,965	12.8
$25,000 to $34,999	13,519,242	12.8
$35,000 to $49,999	17,446,272	16.5
$50,000 to $74,999	20,540,604	19.5
$75,000 to $99,999	10,799,245	10.2
$100,000 to $149,999	8,147,826	7.7
$150,000 to $199,999	2,322,038	2.2
$200,000 or more	2,502,675	2.4
Totals	**105,539,122**	**100**

smaller than those found in the United States, and their members live among largely mixed communities, whereas in the United States, Jamaicans tend to make up a larger percentage of the communities in which they live.

• Study Questions •

1. Where does Jamaica rank among the countries that send immigrants to the United States?

2. What U.S. city has the largest concentration of Jamaican Americans?

3. What field occupies the largest percentage of Jamaican Americans?

6

We're Gonna Make It

When Jamaicans come to North America, they bring with them a picture of America that has been influenced by the media, films, stories, and music. In addition to being able to buy homes, cars, nice clothes, and other symbols of "the American Dream," many Jamaican immigrants believe that if you work hard and get an education, you will be given the opportunity to improve and achieve in life. This chapter focuses on the ways in which Jamaican Americans have worked to "make it" in Canada and the United States through education, employment, and participation in civic life.

EDUCATION: MOVING FORWARD IN LIFE

Education has always been highly valued in Jamaican society, because it is one of the main ways people can "develop" themselves and "move forward in life," in the words of Jamaicans.

Indeed, part of the reason that the Jamaican communities in the United States and Canada have become so large reflects the specialized skills and education that many Jamaicans (and especially Jamaican women) have earned and use to find jobs in business, health care, and education, as well as state, local, and national government.

Successful children of Jamaican immigrants describe their parents' encouragement to work hard, get good grades, and listen to their teachers. Many Jamaican-American parents also stress the importance of discipline and respect for teachers and others in positions of authority in the classroom, and parents in some of the more economically disadvantaged Caribbean neighborhoods have welcomed efforts by various New York school districts to recruit teachers from Jamaica and other Caribbean islands. Although some Jamaican-American parents keep their children in public schools, others send their children to private schools attended mainly by children from the Caribbean islands. One popular school for Jamaican Americans is St. Marks Academy, located in Crown Heights, New York. Like many Jamaican schools, St. Marks Academy stresses discipline and requires its students to wear uniforms.[11]

Members of New York's Jamaican-American community have taken advantage of the City University of New York (CUNY) system, which includes 11 colleges located throughout greater New York. CUNY is the largest public urban university in the United States and has traditionally been accessible to individuals of all races and classes because of its central location and relatively low tuition. CUNY's proximity to Caribbean neighborhoods and its partnership with the New York public schools have helped many Jamaican Americans attend the university. CUNY also boasts a number of prestigious graduates, including former Secretary of State Colin Powell, who graduated from CUNY with a degree in geology in 1958. (See sidebar, this chapter.) Former City Councilwoman Una Clarke, the first Caribbean woman to serve in the New York City legislature, also

Former Secretary of State Colin Powell is the son of two Jamaican immigrants. His father, Luther Theophilus Powell, immigrated to the United States in 1920, while his mother, Maud Ariel Powell, followed suit three years later.

teaches as an adjunct professor in the CUNY system. (See Chapter 9.) A number of reports have suggested that the Jamaican-American commitment to education has paid off—children of West Indian immigrants in the United States often have more years of schooling and, in some instances, even higher incomes than African-American and Euro-American children.

BUILDING COMMUNITY

As do citizens of Jamaica, Jamaican Americans dream of owning their own homes. Home ownership is an important goal for a number of reasons. Many Jamaican-American parents find comfort in having a stable place to live and raise their children, a place where they can control who enters their house and yard and where no one has the right to tell them what to do, how to keep their house, or how to raise their children. Home ownership is also an important investment that can be used to help finance new businesses and support their children's education.

In New York City, Jamaican immigrants traditionally lived with other West Indians in Harlem and the Bedford-Stuyvesant neighborhood of Brooklyn. In the late 1960s and early 1970s, Euro-American and Jewish families living in the East Flatbush and Flatbush neighborhoods of Brooklyn began to move to the suburbs, and Jamaican Americans and other West Indian

COLIN POWELL

General Colin Powell, former secretary of state under President George W. Bush (2001–2005), was born on April 5, 1937. His parents, Luther Theophilus Powell and Maud Ariel Powell, immigrated to New York City from Jamaica and raised young Colin in the Hunts Point neighborhood in the South Bronx. He attended New York City public schools and later the City College of New York (CCNY), where he received a bachelor's degree in geology. He also earned an MBA (Master's of Business Administration) degree from George Washington University.

During his years at CCNY, Powell joined the Reserve Officers' Training Corps (ROTC). After achieving the rank of second lieutenant after graduation, he quickly moved up the ranks and became a decorated officer. (He received the Defense Distinguished Service Medal, the Bronze Star Medal, and the Purple Heart.) He participated in the Vietnam War and rose to command a battalion in Korea and the 2nd Brigade of the 101st Airborne Division in Europe. He also served as the commander-in-chief of forces command at Fort McPherson, Georgia. In 1993, Powell received an Honorary Knighthood (Knight Commander of the Bath) from the queen of England. When Powell retired from the U.S. Army, also in 1993, his admirers noted his moderate attitude and desire for diplomacy over military force.

Americans bought their family homes. Although many middle-class Jamaican Americans have moved to Queens, the West Indian grocery stores, restaurants, and other shops in Flatbush make it the most West Indian neighborhood in New York, and Jamaican Americans comprise one of the largest groups within that community.

Despite their dreams of home and business ownership, many Jamaican Americans find it difficult to obtain reasonable house loans through banks, mainly because of their lack

Powell first entered politics in 1972–73, when he became a White House Fellow under President Richard Nixon. Later, as a general in the U.S. Army, he served as the National Security Advisor to President Ronald Reagan from 1987 to 1989. He became the twelfth chairman of the Joint Chiefs of Staff (1989–1993) under both President George H.W. Bush and President Bill Clinton.

When General Colin Powell was appointed and confirmed secretary of state in 2001, he became the highest-ranking African American in any U.S. administration. Not only was this an impressive personal achievement after 35 years of military service and participation in numerous Republican administrations, but it was also an important milestone for African Americans in the United States. As a member of the Board of Trustees of Howard University and of the Board of Directors of the United Negro College Fund, Powell has often stated that he hoped his participation in both the military and government will inspire other African Americans.

It is clear that Powell's role as U.S. secretary of state paved the way for Dr. Condoleezza Rice, who became the sixty-sixth secretary of state on January 26, 2005, and the highest-ranking African-American woman in any U.S. administration. Powell often attributes his success to his Jamaican parents, whom he describes as supportive and hardworking.

of initial capital, but also because of prejudice in the banking industry. For this reason, Jamaican Americans sometimes come together to create local partners groups—small groups of individuals who help each other save money for large purchases such as mortgage down payments or cars. Regularly giving a set sum of money to the banker in the group, individuals can "draw" (or withdraw) their portion of money when they need it. Because the contributors have been giving money to the banker (and paying the banker a small fee for keeping the money), by the time they receive their part of the money, it has grown into a significant amount. These associations, which are common throughout Jamaica, provide critical capital for immigrants who are not eligible for or are refused loans. They help Jamaican Americans meet traditional down payments for homes and also pay their monthly mortgages.

In Canada, Jamaicans typically settle in residential areas with other West Indians in Ontario, specifically in the greater Toronto area. One of the most popular areas for Jamaicans is "Little Jamaica," located along Eglington, between Keele and Allen roads. In Little Jamaica, there are numerous Jamaican and Caribbean churches, restaurants, grocery stores, and shops, which sell primarily to Jamaican Canadians and other immigrants from the West Indies. Jamaicans also live in the communities of York and Scarborough.

Religion also brings together Jamaicans and other West Indians in Canada. West Indian church networks provided avenues for first-generation Jamaicans to find housing in the face of racial discrimination. They also helped with immigration documents and references. As Frances Henry describes it, "One of the main arenas for networking takes place within the church . . . information about newcomers ['just comes'] flows within the religious network. Help is always offered in finding accommodation and employment."[12] Although the church is losing its younger members, who prefer to get together with other Jamaicans and West Indians in music clubs (see the discussion of Pastor Orim Meikle in Chapter 9, however), most first-generation Jamaican women's social activity centers around the church attended by other West Indians.[13] Many Jamaicans in Canada prefer attending church with other Jamaicans and West Indians, because they share similar beliefs and styles of worship.

"GET UP, STAND UP"

Perhaps the most profound achievement of Jamaican Americans has been their role in fighting racism and other inequalities in North American society. The least celebrated Jamaican Americans sometimes work as domestics in New York and New Jersey homes, caring for other people's children. They also work as nurses, who care for sick patients and nurture them back to health, or as restaurant owners, or as teachers in local schools. They transgress the boundaries of racism and inequality on a day-to-day level in their workplaces and go about their daily lives trying to "live good" (or "get along"), in the words of Jamaicans, with others.

Prominent Jamaican Americans have joined forces with African Americans to fight for the civil rights of all members of American and Canadian society.[14] Some Jamaican Americans have challenged racism directly. Marcus Garvey developed the Universal Negro Improvement Association (see Chapter 2). Harry Belafonte was involved in the civil rights movement and the changing role of African Americans in entertainment (see Chapter 9). Minister Louis Farakkhan currently leads the Nation of Islam, a radical and controversial religious, social, and political organization that seeks to uplift the situation of blacks around the world. Other Jamaican Americans, such as Colin Powell and New York City Council member Una Clarke, who supported the Reverend Jesse Jackson's quests for the Democratic presidential nomination in 1984 and 1988, have worked to challenge and change the structure of U.S. society from within the system.

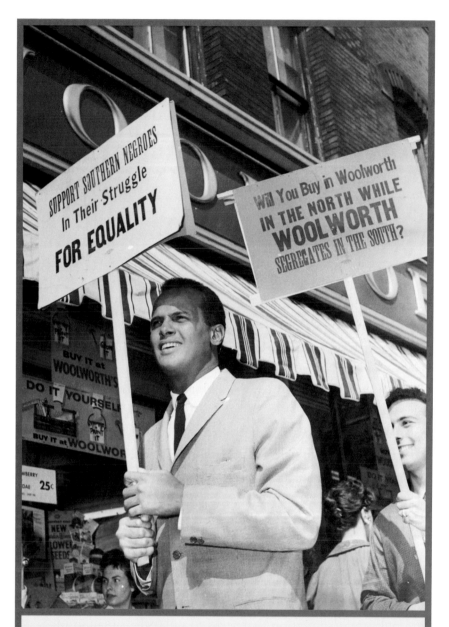

Although born in the United States, actor and musician Harry Belafonte lived in Jamaica with his mother for four years during his youth. Throughout his life, he has been an advocate for civil rights and humanitarian causes. Belafonte is pictured here in 1960 protesting the Woolworth store's policy of segregating their lunch counters.

CONCLUSION

Jamaican Americans have earned a reputation as a patient, hardworking, and achievement-oriented community that has struggled to live the American dream in North America. Some individuals have followed the traditions of earlier Jamaican immigrants, such as Marcus Garvey, who established radical groups to fight racism in North America. Others, such as Colin Powell, have moved through the ranks to challenge "the system" from within. Many ordinary citizens have questioned the situation slowly and steadily through their daily interactions with others in the workplace and in the community.

Not all Jamaican Americans agree about how to go about achieving change. Harry Belafonte has been very critical of former Secretary of State Colin Powell's involvement in Iraq, and many people have argued that Louis Farrakhan and the Nation of Islam's beliefs and descriptions of Euro-Americans as "white devils" have done more to harm the fight against racism and inequality than to help it. Whatever route Jamaican immigrants have chosen to take, their presence has profoundly changed American and Canadian societies, paving the way for racial equality for Jamaican Americans and African Americans alike.

• Study Questions •

1. What factors have brought Jamaican Americans closer together?

2. Who is Colin Powell?

3. How have Jamaican Americans been able to build a community in the United States?

7

Many Rivers to Cross

In the last chapter, we discussed the successes that Jamaican Americans have achieved in building and rebuilding communities in North America through education and employment, and by changing some of the beliefs of citizens in the United States and Canada. Yet, there are also other elements of life in North America that Jamaican Americans continue to struggle with as they adjust to living and raising their children and grandchildren in a new country. This chapter focuses on the problems and challenges of Jamaican Americans in North America and some of the ways that the Jamaican-American community is trying to cope with these difficulties.

"NO WOMAN NO CRY"

In the late 1960s and early 1970s, many upper- and middle-class North American women moved into the workplace. This left middle-class women with a quandary concerning the care of their children and the daily chores at home, such as cleaning and cooking. Jamaican women were recruited during this era to work as nannies and domestic workers. The most valuable and well-paid nannies were those who could live in the households full time, often in an extra or guest room, and had few children or other responsibilities outside of work. As sociologist Nancy Foner has shown, Jamaican women who come to the United States and Canada to take jobs as nannies often leave their children behind with their sisters, mothers, or other family members while they establish themselves in North America.[15] This practice, often called child-shifting, has been a common practice for many women who lived in rural Jamaica and had to travel to Kingston (the capital of Jamaica) and other Jamaican towns for work.

For most mothers, child-shifting was seen as a temporary solution during an uncertain time, and they worked hard so that they could "send for" their children under the immigrant acts' family reunification programs. A number of factors contributed to the continued separation of Jamaican-American mothers and their children in Jamaica. In the first instance, and particularly for those children under the age of five, day care was too expensive for Jamaican nannies working in the boroughs of New York and elsewhere. In addition, many women knew that the apartments and other homes that they could potentially afford were located in low-income neighborhoods, with poor school districts. Many mothers therefore felt that they could better provide for their children by earning enough money in the United States and Canada to pay for private schools in Jamaica.

While they were away, mothers sent remittances (the money they earned outside of Jamaica that is then sent back to that country) to support their children and other relatives. Remittances are used to pay children's school fees, rent, and other expenses,

Many Jamaican mothers work in the United States so that they can pay for their children to attend private schools in Jamaica. Pictured here are schoolchildren taking a test in a private school in Ocho Rios, Jamaica.

and to help out the family members caring for their children while they are working. Remittances have become an important part of Jamaican Americans' lives as well as the larger Jamaican economy, with some reports noting that just as much money is sent back to Jamaica by families living in the United States, Canada, and elsewhere as the entire country earns in tourism, one of Jamaica's most important and lucrative industries.

In addition to remittances, families living abroad also send barrels filled with rice, oil, clothing, shoes, and other valuable consumer items from the United States and Canada to Jamaica. One woman describes what she sends to Jamaica:

Because if you go down to the wharf [in Kingston, Jamaica] now, the wharf is full . . . you see most children are on holiday now they parents send down food and things like that for them because it's much better and it's much cheaper. Because the amount of money we have been spending and using to buy food to pack the barrel, if we bring that money out here to come and buy food, that can only serve us for a week. And we bring food that can serve us fi [for] three to four months. And we buy everything. The only thing we don't bring down is saltfish. [We bring] drinks, everything for the kids, soap, everything.[16]

The practice has become so common in Jamaica that the label "barrel children" is used to refer to the children whose parents send barrels of clothing, shoes, and food during the many years that they are away.

The fact that child-shifting is a long-standing practice in Jamaica shows the flexibility of Jamaican families in coping with poverty and other difficult situations. Many parents and children recognize important economic benefits of working abroad, because the money earned often supports entire families or pays a child's school fees and expenses for the year. (After a child reaches the age of 12, families must pay tuition for each student enrolled in school.)

In the studies of cell-phone usage in Jamaica,[17] a number of children whose parents worked in the United States and Canada while they were growing up reported that they missed their mothers during critical teenage years. Kids whose parents now work outside of Jamaica often save up their lunch or "pocket money," skipping lunches or walking a few extra miles at the end of the school day, in order to make a phone call to their mother or father living abroad. The feelings of loneliness and worry associated with the parents' absence leave many families questioning the long-term effects of these economic advantages.

Oftentimes, Jamaican children must live with their grandparents or other relatives when their parents work abroad. Known as child-shifting, this practice has become widespread in Jamaica.

"SO MUCH TROUBLE IN THE WORLD"

Although some parents keep their children in Jamaica while they work in North America, other parents are ultimately able to unite their family and bring their children to the United States and Canada. The demands of work and the expense of day care and housing bring new hardships for parents who try to meet the demands of caring for their children and "making it" in North American society. Unlike in Jamaica, where family, friends, and neighbors watch each others' kids as favors, in urban Canada and the United States, Jamaican-American parents often find the situation difficult because people tend to keep to themselves.

For a variety of reasons, young Jamaican-American men in cities such as New York, Washington, D.C., and Toronto have become particularly vulnerable to the influence of gangs, which are often referred to as "posses." Posses have been depicted in the media, as well as in popular culture, as a specifically Jamaican social structure emerging alongside the trade in illegal drugs and arms. Although the exact origins of posses is not certain (some argue that their involvement in the drug trade is linked to the CIA, and others argue that Jamaican politicians are involved), posses continue to lure many young Jamaican Americans who express frustration and helplessness. In many instances, these difficulties are tied to the day-to-day experience of racism that young Jamaican-American youth face as they attempt to find jobs and earn money.

In contrast to media portrayals that show Jamaican-American (and black) youth involvement in crime as natural, the appeal of gangs, or posses, among Jamaican-American youth must be understood within the wider context of North American society, where not all people are actually provided with equal access to employment and quality educational opportunities. For many youths, joining gangs seems to provide individuals who grew up in less than ideal circumstances access to the symbols of success (for example, BMWs, gold jewelry, and so on) and power (guns and related violence), which otherwise seem to be out of their reach.

The appeal of gangs and crime is not just about money, designer clothes, cars, and other objects. It is also about asserting a sense of belonging and respect. Like many African-American men of their generation, young Jamaican-American men, especially, feel that they will never possess a good job or achieve their goals in life. Disillusioned with "the system," as it is called, Jamaican-American youth are comforted by spending time with others who understand their experience.

Unfortunately, many young men involved in gangs have lost their lives, gone to prison, or been deported. Deportation is the sending back of people convicted of crime and violence to their country of birth. The deportation of people who were born in Jamaica but effectively spent their lives in the United States has also impacted Jamaica, which already has a high homicide rate. Some of the individuals who are deported report that they were unfairly accused of the crimes and, in some cases, they may be justified, because African-American men are overrepresented in North American (especially U.S.) prisons. When they are deported, they are restricted from living in the U.S. and Canada, where they grew up. Without strong relationships with relatives in Jamaica, they often have difficulty adjusting to life in Jamaica and finding a place to live, and they feel forced to return to a life of crime. Many Jamaicans blame their high homicide rate

In 1995, Louis Farrakhan, the leader of the Nation of Islam and the son of a Jamaican taxi driver from New York, organized the Million Man March. Designed to increase black involvement in volunteerism and community activism, the march was held on October 16 of that year in Washington, D.C.

(1,600 people were murdered in Jamaica in 2005) on the deportees sent back from the United States, the United Kingdom, and Canada.

The church and other individuals have recognized the dire situation of Jamaican-American (and African-American) youths and have attempted to create alternative support networks. For example, Louis Farrakhan, the leader of the Nation of Islam and the son of a Jamaican taxi driver living in New York, organized the Million Man March in Washington, D.C., on October 16, 1995. The march, perhaps the largest gathering of black men in American history, was envisioned as a symbol of protest as well as unity within the African-American community. Many people were uncomfortable with Farrakhan's role in the march, given the Nation of Islam's involvement in violence and Farrakhan's negativity toward Jews and other ethnic groups. Other, less radical visionaries, such as Pastor Orim Meikle in Toronto and New York City Council member Yvette D. Clarke, have stressed education and have tried to revitalize and reform many of the neighborhoods where Jamaican-American and African-American youths live.

CONCLUSION

Although Jamaican Americans have achieved success in many ways, they also face many challenges as they enter the United States and Canada. For women especially, the ties of family and children prove to be a difficult challenge as they come to North American cities to take advantage of economic opportunities and to begin to build a life for their families in North America. Men, and particularly young men, have difficulty finding employment and turn to gangs for social and emotional support. As we discuss further in the following chapter, these difficulties are often shared with members of the wider African-American and West Indian communities in Canada and the United States.

GROWING UP IN LOS ANGELES

Alton McIntyre, known to his friends as "Ska-man," arrived in Jamaica in 2001 to "cool off," after having run into trouble with the law for the third time. McIntyre was born in Los Angeles, the third son of Deanne, a Jamaican immigrant who worked for 20 years as a cleaner in a major recording studio—without ever getting her papers in order. Deanne had left two other sons in Jamaica, with her sister, because, according to her, the sons' father was "no good" and drank.

Alton's father was not happy to be presented with a son and played very little role in his upbringing. When Alton was 14, Deanne decided to return to Jamaica and, against Alton's wishes, left him with his father in downtown Los Angeles. She thought he would have better opportunities in the United States than he would in Jamaica. For several years, Alton was fearful of having to share the same room with a man who did not want him. Alton had been doing well at school up until this point, but then his grades began to fall and he felt there was no future for him even if he did well. "There was no room for weakness out there, it was a hard life,"* he recalled later.

Alton began to run with one of the local posses, finding both friendship and strong rules of honor. "Everyone has a gun out there, without it you get no respect. Everyone knew Jamaicans were tough and I was a strong Jamaican."** Alton's main memory of Los Angeles was living with the knowledge that you could be attacked at any moment, even for something that you knew nothing about. In Jamaica, Alton also finds it hard to fit in, because there he is viewed as a "showy American." Because he is unlikely to return to where he was born, Ska-man is now running a restaurant in Jamaica, where he is hoping to attract American, Canadian, and European tourists.

---

*Quote from interview with coauthor (Garner, 2005).
**Ibid.

• Study Questions •

1. Name some of the difficulties that Jamaican Americans encounter in the United States and Canada.

2. How are these difficulties experienced differently by women and men?

3. Why do some women choose to leave their children behind with relatives in Jamaica while they work in the United States and Canada?

4. Do you think that the economic gains outweigh the sacrifices for Jamaican families?

5. What are some of the reasons that some Jamaican-American boys get involved in gangs and crime?

6. How have members of the African-American and Jamaican-American communities tried to lure young men away from gangs? Give examples.

8

One Love

When Jamaicans begin their journey to Canada or the United States, they carry with them images and ideas about what life will be like there. These images have been influenced by their upbringing, education, status, and life experience. Images of North American life in television shows, news programs, films, videos, music, and other media also play an important role in shaping the ideas many Jamaicans have about the United States and Canada and, in turn, the ways in which Jamaicans imagine their own future lives in American and Canadian society. At the same time, the process of migration and the new places, people, and experiences Jamaican immigrants encounter also influence their views of North American society. This chapter discusses the many ways in which Jamaican immigrants develop ties and a sense of belonging in the United States and Canada.

ETHNIC IDENTITIES: JAMAICANS AS WEST INDIAN AMERICANS AND CARIBBEAN AMERICANS

Twenty-four islands and at least three countries comprise the Caribbean region and share a history of slavery, colonialism, religious practices, and geography. Caribbean islanders have a long history of migration within the region, and Caribbean governments have made a continued effort to create a single Caribbean legal and economic system, such as the Caribbean Court of Justice and CARICOM. Even so, Jamaicans did not interact with other West Indian or Caribbean peoples on a daily basis. Many Jamaicans did not recognize the similarities between themselves and Trinidadians, Cayman Islanders, St. Lucians, and Bajans (from Barbados) and began to see themselves not just as Jamaicans but also as individuals of Caribbean or West Indian origin until they immigrated to U.S. and Canadian cities or towns.

The sense of feeling Caribbean or West Indian is particular to each migration destination. For example, New York has been an important city for West Indians in the United States. Each year, the Caribbean-American community holds the West Indian American Day Carnival in Brooklyn, New York, in September, over Labor Day weekend. Carnival is a Trinidadian tradition during which members of the community dress in masks and elaborate costumes, walk in parades, and hold music, dance, and other competitions. The carnival tradition has expanded to welcome new musical styles, such as Jamaican reggae, and activities from other West Indian islands.

Although carnivals are often the most prominent West Indian cultural activity, the Jamaicans' love of cricket and soccer has also influenced North American life. In 1977, soccer fans were thrilled when the West Indian Jets Soccer Club, founded by Jamaicans and other West Indians living in Chicago, represented the state of Illinois in the United States Cup.

The West Indian American Day Carnival is held annually in Brooklyn, New York, on Labor Day weekend. The celebration is the largest Carnival in North America and one of New York's largest ethnic festivals.

In New York, Jamaicans represent the largest West Indian population. In Miami and South Florida, however, Jamaicans join a wider Caribbean community, which includes Cubans and Haitians. Many community groups and celebrations reflect this pan-Caribbean sense of identity. For example, in 2004, Caribefest was held in Miami to celebrate the various cultures of the Caribbean. The festival involved music, dance, food, and crafts from the traditions of the Anglophone (English-speaking), Hispanic (Spanish-speaking), and Francophone (French-speaking) Caribbean. Festival-goers could experience Haitian music alongside Jamaican deejays. Toronto holds a similar festival, called Caribana, each summer, which now incorporates traditional and contemporary musicians and artists from Trinidad, Guyana, Jamaica, Brazil, and the Bahamas.

RACIAL IDENTITIES: JAMAICANS AND AFRICAN AMERICANS

In contrast to Canada, where there is a relatively small African-Canadian community, Afro-Jamaican immigrants in the United States are often overlooked as part of the larger country's African-American community. Despite sharing a historical past such as the transatlantic slave trade, culturally, Jamaicans are not the same as African Americans and they possess a different understanding of race than what is commonly held in the United States. In Jamaican society, the meaning of race is determined through a variety of factors, including facial features, skin color, and hair type, as well as socioeconomic status, and Jamaicans recognize a variety of shades of color in their descriptions of individuals. By contrast, in North America, race is a more rigid concept tied much more closely to biology: Any person with a small amount of African ancestry is viewed as African American. For example, whereas in Jamaica a woman who has mixed ancestry, a lighter complexion, and straight hair might be described as "brown" or even "white" in some cases, the same individual would be described as "black" or African American in the United States. These different perspectives on race mean that although Jamaicans do not necessarily see themselves as African American, the attitudes and assumptions that many other Americans hold about African-American families or other cultural features are often projected onto Jamaican immigrants. Indeed, many fair- and brown-skinned Jamaican immigrants contend that it is only once they arrive in North America that they understand what it means to be "black."

Many Jamaican immigrants find that they are culturally different from African Americans, but the assumptions held by the wider American society alter their experience within

During New York City's 1989 mayoral election, Jamaican Americans overwhelmingly supported Democratic candidate David Dinkins. Pictured here in 2004, Dinkins was New York's first and only African-American mayor and served one term in office (1989–1993).

American society and their relationship with African Americans. Jamaican Americans have increasingly formed political alliances with African Americans by supporting candidates such as David Dinkins, who became the first African-American mayor of New York City in 1989. In addition, Jamaican Americans have rallied behind Reverend Jesse Jackson's bids for the U.S. presidency in 1984 and 1988 and have utilized and fought alongside African Americans to maintain affirmative action programs that provide opportunities for historically disenfranchised minorities in the United States. Former District 40 (NY) City Councilwoman Una Clarke, a Jamaican immigrant, has appealed to African-American voters in her district of Flatbush.

TRANSNATIONAL IDENTITIES: HOMETOWN AND NATIONAL ASSOCIATIONS

When they first arrived in North America, many Jamaican immigrants believed that their stay in North America would be temporary—that the money and degrees attained through work and schooling abroad were designed to enhance their opportunities and status when they eventually returned to their island home. The focus on returning to Jamaica meant that many of the early Jamaican immigrants created community organizations and associations that addressed issues in Jamaica. One of the most prominent organizations was the Jamaica Progressive League of New York (JPL). Established in 1936, the JPL was originally created (1) to help improve the working and living conditions in Jamaica and (2) to assist in fostering independence from Britain. By the time the majority of the post-1965 immigrants became involved in the JPL, Jamaica was finally independent and a number of the leaders of the JPL in New York had returned to Jamaica. Post-1965 immigrants who joined the JPL shifted their focus to returning the People's National Party (PNP) to power in Jamaica, a goal that was attained in 1972, when the PNP won the election.

Because of the socialist orientation of the PNP under Prime Minister Michael Manley, and the United States' stance against Communism and Fidel Castro's Cuban government, the JPL's affiliation with the PNP became increasingly difficult for Jamaicans living in the United States. Consequently, the JPL began to lose prominence among members of the Jamaican-American community in New York.

Although the JPL and other organizations concerned with the political, social, and economic situation in Jamaica remain, today Jamaicans (and other immigrants) no longer feel that acceptance within American or Canadian society means that they must choose between being Jamaican or North American. Instead, they hold what is sometimes called a transnational identity. Today, the widespread access to telephones and relatively inexpensive air travel, as well as the increasing number of house phones and cell phones in Jamaica, make it possible for Jamaican Americans to keep in touch with their friends and family in Jamaica. Groups such as the National Council of Jamaicans and Supportive Organizations in Canada, Inc., have been involved in youth development projects to motivate and teach leadership skills to Jamaican youth in Canada. Members of these organizations can therefore be committed to improving the conditions of Jamaicans living in Canada and the United States and at the same time be involved with and help their friends and family in Jamaica.

THE SECOND GENERATION

The sense of belonging felt by second-generation Jamaicans continues to be important for understanding the dynamics of migration. In the past, scholars of migration argued that children and grandchildren of the original immigrants would be assimilated, or absorbed into, American and Canadian societies by the third generation because of the lack of exposure to their parents' country of origin.

The situation now seems more complicated. For example, although many first-generation immigrants maintain an attachment to Jamaica, second-generation Jamaican Americans often possess a different perspective. Because they attend school with African Americans and typically live in African-American neighborhoods, many second-generation Jamaicans feel they can relate more to the experiences of African Americans than they can to Jamaica. For these youths, who might never have even visited Jamaica, the island remains the site of their parents' youth and their own ancestry, but Jamaica itself seems to have little impact on their day-to-day lives in Canada and the United States. These youths may tend to feel more like African Americans or African Canadians than they do Jamaican Americans.

Other scholars have argued that the recent support of multiculturalism, or the respect of cultural differences in countries such as Canada, has enabled Jamaicans living in North America to recognize the importance of their Jamaican and Caribbean or West Indian ancestry, and thus many of the first generation's children and grandchildren want to learn about their history by visiting Jamaica. In addition, there has been a long practice of sending children to Jamaica to live with family for their primary- and secondary-school education (see Chapters 6 and 7). For this reason, the melting of the second and third generations of Jamaican immigrants within the African-American or African-Canadian community at the expense of their Jamaican ancestry is no longer a necessity.

CONCLUSION

Despite the aforementioned exceptions, most first-, second, and third-generation Jamaican Americans express attachment to Jamaica, as well as affiliation with African Americans and other West Indian or Caribbean peoples. In arenas such as schooling, Jamaican Americans may join in the struggle to fight against racism. By contrast, with their aims toward making a living and taking advantage of economic opportunities, the eagerness of many first-generation Jamaican Americans to work, even for poor wages, may hurt the attempts of African Americans to earn larger salaries.

On the other hand, when choosing a church, Jamaican Americans may join a denomination with other West Indians who share similar practices and styles of worship. When issues or

CHINESE JAMAICANS IN CANADA

In the mid-1800s, the Chinese immigrated to Jamaica to work on sugar plantations and railroads as indentured laborers. They came predominantly from a minority population in southern China, where a dialect called Hakka was spoken.

The Chinese-Jamaican community grew little by little and became particularly prominent in the small grocery business, which bartered and extended credit for staples of the Jamaican diet. Later generations continued this tradition by establishing themselves in groceries and other forms of commerce. One example is the Chen family, who owns the 22 Superplus groceries located throughout Jamaica. Although Chinese Jamaicans remain a small, tight-knit community, they live side by side with and have intermarried with the larger population.

Dancehall entertainer Sean Paul is one such member of this community; his father is white and Portuguese, and his mother is half Chinese Jamaican. Also consider third-generation Chinese Jamaican Michael Lee-Chin, the CEO of AIC Diversified Canada Split Corporation and one of Canada's wealthiest citizens, whose parents were half Chinese and half Afro-Jamaican.

The economic success of the minority Chinese Jamaicans has created some tension in Jamaica, particularly during the political, social, and economic turmoil of the 1960s and 1970s. In what is sometimes referred to as the Chinese-

events directly impact Jamaica, such as in 2004 when Hurricane Ivan passed over the island, many Jamaican Americans rallied together to send money, food, clothing, and other items to assist their friends, families, and communities in Jamaica. Whether Jamaican Americans will eventually assimilate within the wider American and Canadian societies is no longer the important question. Rather, we should understand where, how, and when they express the many facets of being Jamaican American.

Jamaican exodus, the Chinese-Jamaican community fell from 11,781 in 1970 to 5,320 in 1980, when large numbers of Chinese Jamaicans moved to cities such as Toronto and Miami. Like the Afro-Jamaican community in the United States, who are often viewed as African American, Chinese Jamaicans are often confused with Asian Americans and Asian Canadians, because they "look" Chinese or Asian rather than what many see as typically Jamaican.

Although many Chinese Jamaicans have retained and adapted cooking and social practices from their Chinese heritage, their accents, taste in food, dress, and manner often appear strange or out of place within the wider Asian community in North America. In addition, the majority of Chinese Jamaicans have converted to Christianity, predominantly Catholicism, since leaving the shores of China, and they feel that they share little in common with the older generations of Chinese in Toronto or the newer generations of Hong Kong Chinese, who immigrated to the United States and Canada in the 1990s.

Some Chinese Jamaicans have responded to their new environments by establishing greater connections to their Hakka ancestry. Others have created Jamaican-Chinese networks and neighborhoods in places such as the Toronto suburb of Markham.

• Study Questions •

1. Describe the three most common ways that Jamaican Americans develop a sense of belonging in North America.

2. How is the experience of Jamaican immigrants different in Canada and the United States?

3. How is the Jamaican-American community in Toronto different from the Jamaican-American community in New York? Describe some of the ways that they are different.

4. How is the Jamaican-American community in New York different from the Jamaican community in Miami? Describe some of the ways that they are different.

5. How has the presence of African Americans in the United States affected Jamaican immigrants?

6. How does the second-generation experience differ from the first-generation experience?

7. How are the experiences of Jamaican Americans in the United States similar to those of Chinese Jamaicans in Canada? How are they different?

9

Legend

In the previous chapters, we discussed the processes of migration and the ways in which Jamaican Americans became part of society in Canada and the United States. For many Americans and Canadians who do not live and work with Jamaicans in their day-to-day lives, the only way they are exposed to people of Jamaican descent is through popular culture. This chapter focuses on the many ways in which Jamaicans and Jamaican Americans have influenced American and Canadian culture and society, and how they have changed the face of politics, sports, music, and entertainment.

MUSIC

Music has always been at the fore of Jamaican society. The ability of music (and musicians) to travel has allowed Jamaican and African-American musical styles to influence one another. What we know today as "rapping" in hip-hop music mixes "toasting," or talking over a musical beat or rhythm, in African-American culture with the "toasting" practices of Jamaican deejays, who use toasting to energize and involve the audience at parties and performances. For example, hip-hop artist Shaggy was born in Jamaica but immigrated with his family to Flatbush, New York, as a child. Shaggy later joined the U.S. Marine Corps to fight in Operation Desert Storm and, after his return, became a force in hip-hop and reggae through songs such as "Oh Carolina" and "It Wasn't Me."

More recently, musicians such as Damian Marley, the son of Bob Marley and former Miss World 1976 Cindy Breakspeare, have combined the Jamaican genres of reggae and dancehall with hip-hop. Marley, who lives in Miami, Florida, and Kingston, Jamaica, won two Grammys, the first for Best Reggae Album for *Welcome to Jamrock* and the second for Best Urban/Alternative Performance for the song "Welcome To Jamrock." One of the founding members of the Black Eyed Peas, will.i.am, has incorporated some of the sounds of his Jamaican-American heritage by uniquely fusing the genres of rap, reggae, alternative, and hip-hop. will.i.am grew up in Los Angeles and formed the group in 1989 with fellow band member apl.de.ap; the group won five Grammy Awards between 2004 and 2006.

ENTERTAINMENT

Jamaican Americans have made such a large contribution to entertainment in North America—from film, television, and theater to music and modeling—that Jamaican-American actress Sheryl Lee Ralph founded the International Jamerican Film and Music Festival, which was created "to showcase artistic achievement, market products, foster relationships, discuss the future of the industry, as well as learn and teach through seminars, exhibitions and conversation." Each year, the Marcus

Garvey Lifetime Achievement Award is presented to successful Jamaican Americans, including in 1999, when it was presented to Harry Belafonte.[18]

Other Jamaican Americans are also prominent in North American music and entertainment. Ziggy Marley, the eldest son of Bob Marley, and his wife, Rita Marley, sing the theme song for the PBS children's program *Arthur*. Corbin Bleu, whose father is Jamaican, plays Nathan in the Discovery Kids series *Flight 29 Down*. Bleu is also the lead character Izzy Daniels in the 2007 Disney Channel movie *Jump*. Roger Cross plays the character Curtis Manning on the popular series *24*. Jamaican-born Grace Jones, an actress, musician, and model, played May Day in the 1985 James Bond movie *A View to a Kill*. Model and actor Tyson Beckford, whose father is Afro-Jamaican and mother is Chinese Jamaican, became the face of Ralph Lauren in 1993 and has been named one of the 50 most beautiful people in the world by *People* magazine.

Perhaps the most famous Jamaican-American entertainer is Harry Belafonte. Born in Harlem, New York, in 1927, Belafonte lived with his Jamaican mother in a small village in Jamaica between the ages of 8 and 12. Returning to New York in 1939 to attend George Washington High School, he finished school and joined the U.S. Navy. After serving in the navy, Belafonte began to take acting classes and eventually made his way into films such as *Island in the Sun*, a movie about race relations on the island of Grenada. He also wrote and sang the title song. Belafonte's most famous song, the "Banana Boat Song" (sometimes known as "Day-O"), based on a Jamaican calypso song, was released on the album *Calypso* in 1956. The album was the first LP to sell more than 1 million copies.

Belafonte was involved in the civil rights movement in the 1950s and 1960s and was known to be a close friend of Martin Luther King, Jr. He continued to push the boundaries

Model and actor Tyson Beckford grew up in Rochester, New York, and is the son of a Jamaican father and a Jamaican/Chinese-American mother. In 1995, he was named one of *People* magazine's 50 Most Beautiful People.

of blacks and African Americans in the media. He was the first African American to win an Emmy Award for his 1959 TV special "Tonight With Belafonte," and he won a Grammy Award for Lifetime Achievement in 2000. He has also used his fame to draw attention to poverty and inequality as a UNICEF goodwill ambassador, and, since the 1980s, he has focused much of his attention on Africa. In his later years, he has not shied away from controversy—he has vehemently criticized the Bush administration's response to the terrorist attacks of September 11, 2001, as well as fellow Jamaican American and former Secretary of State Colin Powell and current Secretary of State Condoleeza Rice for their involvement in the Bush government.

ATHLETICS

Sports have also always played an important role in Jamaican society, and, not surprisingly, Jamaican Americans have figured prominently in American and Canadian athletic events. Like the Jamaican bobsled team who fought to qualify for the 1988 Olympics despite having little money, second-hand equipment, and very little experience in the snow, Jamaicans and Jamaican Americans pride themselves on competing in a global setting against the odds. (See also the Disney movie *Cool Runnings*, about a Jamaican bobsled team in 1993.) They frequently come to the United States and Canada on athletic scholarships (especially in track and field). From NBA star Patrick Ewing, who was on the first Olympic "Dream Team" with Michael Jordon; baseball player Charles Theodore "Chili" Davis; high-jump champions Milt Ottey and Mark Boswell; and bobsled Olympian Lascelles Brown, Jamaican Americans have strengthened American and Canadian athletics.

In Canada, one of the most important figures in track and field is Jamaican-born Donovan Bailey, who won gold for Canada at the 1996 Atlanta Olympic Games. Competing in the

100-meter event, Bailey set a new world and Olympic record at 9.84 seconds. For Canadian sports, Bailey's achievement was a welcome and much-needed win after the Ben Johnson scandal, which took center stage in the 1988 Summer Olympics in Seoul, South Korea. Johnson, also born in Jamaica, won a gold medal for Canada in the 100-meters but three days later was stripped of his medal after testing positive for steroids. The stripping of his medal was a blow to Canada's pride. Johnson felt the backlash of Canadians through the media, who stopped talking about Johnson as a "Canadian" and started describing him as "Jamaican."

Although Donovan Bailey restored Canada's sporting honor, he, too, was soon enmeshed in controversy. After Bailey's win in the 100-meters in 9.84 seconds, there was speculation that American Michael Johnson actually deserved the title, because his win in the 1996 Olympic 200-meters at the world-record time of 19.32 seconds was technically faster in miles per hour (an average of 9.66 seconds). Bailey and Johnson accepted a challenge to compete for the title "World's Fastest Man" in June 1997. Bailey and Johnson were set to race in the Toronto Skydome, but Johnson pulled out of the race with a quadriceps injury, leaving Bailey to win the title and take the $1.5 million prize. In addition to earning his Olympic gold(s), Bailey was also the anchor for the 4x100-meter relay team that won gold, and later went on to repeat as the world champion in Athens and to set the Canadian record for the 100 meters.

A successful businessman and stock broker before his foray into sprinting, Bailey retired in 2001 and established a business for amateur athletes. He continued his charitable work as a spokesperson for Big Brothers and Sisters of Toronto and the Canadian Cancer Society. He has also been supportive of the new co-world-record-holder, Jamaican Asafa Powell, who shares his time of 9.77 seconds in the 100-meter with American Justin Gatlin.

POLITICS AND ACTIVISM

In earlier chapters, we noted the rise of retired General Colin Powell to secretary of state in the United States and the importance of the position for Jamaican Americans and African Americans alike. In Canada, a number of individuals born in Jamaica have started out in local politics and worked their way into the provincial, state, and federal government. For example, Alvin Curling, representing Scarborough North, was first elected to the Ontario legislature in the provincial election of 1985 and appointed minister of housing. Curling became the first black Canadian to hold a cabinet-level position in Ontario. Curling was later elected speaker of the legislature, in November 2003.

In addition, and unlike within many other immigrant communities, Jamaican-American women have also risen to prominent positions. In Canada, Beverley Salmon became the first black woman to become a Provincial Human Rights Commissioner, and Pamela Appelt was appointed to the Court of Canadian Citizenship; she was the first female judge of Jamaican descent. Dr. Rosemary Brown (1930–2003), a feminist activist and politician, was elected to the provincial legislature of British Columbia in 1972, which made her the first black woman to be a member of a Canadian parliamentary body. She also was a founding member of the Vancouver Status of Women Council and the Vancouver Crisis Center. She was appointed the CEO of MATCH International, a development agency that sought to improve the conditions and living situations of women around the world.

In 1991, in New York City, Una Clarke was elected to the 40th Council District in Brooklyn, an area dominated by immigrants from Jamaica, Trinidad, Haiti, Grenada, and Panama. Clarke was the first Jamaican (and Caribbean) woman to serve as a councilwoman in the city legislature after a long career of local advocacy for women and children in Brooklyn.

In 2001, Clarke's daughter, Yvette D. Clarke, was elected to the New York City Council and has developed an HIV/AIDS Task Force in her district to assist with combating the disease, particularly among youth. She has also been working with neighborhood churches to develop a sense of community, which she believes will reduce crime among young men and women. On November 7, 2006, she was elected to the U.S. House of Representatives for New York's 11th District. Clarke joins Sheila Jackson Lee, a second-generation Jamaican American who was elected in 1995, in the House of Representatives. Jackson Lee, a Democrat, represents Texas's 18th Congressional District.

OTHER CONTRIBUTIONS

Although achievements in music, athletics, and politics receive a great deal of attention, Jamaican Americans have also made a considerable contribution to literature and education. Rachel Manley, for example, won the 1997 Governor General's Literary Award for her book *Drumblair*. The book talks about Manley's childhood with her father, Michael Manley, the prime minister of Jamaica from 1972 to 1980 and again from 1988 to 1992. It also talks about other members of her powerful family, such as her grandparents: Norman Manley, the chief minister of Jamaica (1955 to 1962) and Edna Manley, a celebrated Jamaican artist and social activist.

Other Jamaican Americans have contributed to the spiritual life of their communities. One such individual is Pastor Orim M. Meikle, an evangelist on Canadian radio. Pastor Meikle's television program *Rhema Today* is broadcast in the United States, Canada, and throughout the world. His nondenominational, multiethnic Pentecostal church in Toronto, Rhema Christian Ministries, has grown to 2,000 members and offers a number of programs to help youth struggling with crime and poverty in urban Toronto.

Sheila Jackson Lee, who represents the 18th Congressional District in Texas, has served as a member of the U.S. House of Representatives since 1995. The granddaughter of Jamaican immigrants, Lee was born in Queens, New York, and was recently named one of the 10 most influential legislators in the House of Representatives by *U.S. News and World Report*.

CONCLUSION

Jamaican Americans have played prominent roles in North American society. In music, Jamaican-American talent has fused the sounds of Jamaican mento, calypso, reggae, and dancehall with hip-hop and alternative music. Jamaican-American athletes have reached the pinnacle of success, attaining Olympic gold medals, and commonwealth and world championships. Jamaican-American and Jamaican-Canadian politicians, particularly Jamaican-American women, have reached some of the highest ranks of government in both the United States and Canada, achieving not only "firsts" for Jamaican Americans but also for African Americans and African Canadians.

• Study Questions •

1. How have Jamaican-American musicians influenced the American and Canadian music scenes?

2. How has Harry Belafonte changed the American entertainment industry? Why is he such an important figure for Jamaican Americans?

3. Compare and contrast the lives of Harry Belafonte and retired General Colin Powell. How has each tried to improve life in the United States?

4. Why was Donovan Bailey's Olympic gold medal in 1996 so important to Canada?

5. Name three important Jamaican-American and Jamaican-Canadian politicians and activists. What did each individual do to contribute to American or Canadian society?

6. What role have Jamaican-American women played in North American politics?

10

Positive Vibration

We all inherit different histories. These are the stories and experiences that make us who we are. They can be everyday things, such as the food you always eat at home or on special occasions. Or they can be things that can seem very remote, like slavery and the sugar plantations, but that still have a huge effect on how you see your place in the world. They can be things that seem immediate and important, like what you can do to earn money and what you spend it on, where you live, and the options and opportunities available to you to make your life better. This book has been about the histories and options available to the approximately 800,000 people from Jamaica now living in North America.

JAMAICAN-AMERICAN CULTURE

At the beginning of this book, we introduced four themes important in understanding Jamaican-American culture: food, music, religion, and a willingness to travel to seek better opportunities. These factors all play an important role in the lives of Jamaicans who now live in North America. They provided a starting point from which to learn about Jamaican immigrants, but they are also interwoven within the chapters and topics discussed in this book.

Consequently, if we look at the long history of struggle against slavery and oppression, we will see that one of the driving forces for change rests in religious beliefs and the commitment of ministers and laypeople to protest against injustice. Religious belief is what changed the black consciousness brought by Marcus Garvey into Rastafarianism—a uniquely Jamaican amalgamation of belief and identity. The Bible and hymns have strongly influenced the language of much popular music, particularly reggae. Church networks also play a role in deciding where Jamaicans settle in North America and how they are able to get jobs. Arguably, religious belief also positively affects Jamaican attitudes toward education and also the traditional respect shown to elderly family members. Although church and belief networks often seem to play a conservative role in people's lives, they can also take a radical approach to helping to combat inequality.

During the course of the book, we saw how other elements also played an important role in Jamaican immigration. Many influences were economic: the push factors of lack of work in Jamaica and the pull factors of the job options and earning potential of moving to North America. The demand for qualified and hardworking nurses and other skilled people affected immigration decisions, and the sacrifices people were willing to make to fulfil these roles also affected them. These included leaving their children behind to be cared for by someone else. Many Jamaicans work hard not only for their own gain, but also to be able to send money back to their native country for other family members.

We also saw how important government immigration policies are in determining the numbers and kinds of people who can work in North America. Government policies meant that decisions about immigrants were made on the basis of race, and then later on the types of skills needed in the labor force and on allowing families to live in the same country together. Policy changes also meant that more women than men traveled from Jamaica to North America, and that Canadian and U.S. policies had different effects on immigration. Most recently, we can see the effects of the "War Against Terror," which in trying to protect U.S. citizens, has often ended up limiting immigration from countries almost completely uninvolved in terrorism.

Jamaican immigration has also had a significant impact, both on the host countries and on the immigrants themselves. For instance, during the Harlem Renaissance, new forms of artistic, cultural, and social writing gave voice to a black consciousness for virtually the first time. These forms of cultural expression, which reflect on the experience of being categorized as black in America, have, in turn, added an exceptionally rich strand to the overall cultural heritage of the United States. Jamaican Americans have also contributed strongly to the battle for civil liberties and to the recognition in government that policies based on race are unjust and immoral.

One of the biggest cultural shocks for Jamaicans arriving in North America was that they found themselves categorized as "black" rather than "Jamaican." This category meant little in terms of their own value system and they were sometimes seen as traitors to the "black" cause because they made little distinction between black and white friends. Many, in fact, opted to live in areas deemed white and to share the emphasis given to educational achievement.

In recent decades, part of the response has been to identify themselves as West Indians. Some of this identity confusion brought on by competing cultural systems has meant that

(continues on page 120)

JAMAICAN JERK CHICKEN

"Jerk" is a method of cooking pork and chicken that dates back to the Taino-Arawak Indians who inhabited Jamaica. First, an animal is killed and thoroughly cleaned and gutted. Then, the carcass is "jerked" with a sharp object and the holes stuffed with a variety of spices. The carcass is then placed in a deep pit, lined with stones, and covered with green wood, which, when burned, smokes heavily and adds to the flavor. The results are superb. The meat is not only wonderfully spiced, but also moist and tender.

JERK CHICKEN

1 tbsp. ground allspice	1/4 c. olive oil
1 tbsp. dried leaf thyme	1/4 c. soy sauce
1 1/2 tsp. cayenne pepper	3/4 c. white vinegar
1 1/2 tsp. black pepper	1/2 c. orange juice
1 1/2 tsp. ground sage	1/4 c. fresh lime juice
3/4 tsp. ground nutmeg	1 Scotch Bonnet pepper
3/4 tsp. ground cinnamon	1 c. finely chopped white onion
2 tbsp. salt	3 green onions, finely chopped
2 tbsp. garlic powder	4 (6- to 8-oz.) whole chicken
1 tbsp. sugar	breasts, skinned and boned

In medium-sized bowl, combine the first 10 ingredients, including the sugar. Mixing with wire whisk, slowly add olive oil, soy sauce, vinegar, and orange and lime juices. Use rubber or plastic gloves to prepare hot pepper (jalapeno or serrano may be substituted). Avoid touching face or eyes! Add chopped pepper and chopped onions to marinade; mix well.

Spread 2 cups marinade in glass baking dish. Add chicken to coat in marinade. Cover and marinate at least 1 hour (overnight is best). Reserve 3/4 cup of marinade as a dipping sauce. On grill, cook chicken over medium to high heat 6 minutes each side. Baste with excess drained marinade.*

---

* Available online at *http://www.cooks.com/rec/doc/0,1939,148181-237195,00.html.*

The annual Jamaican Jerk Festival in Miami, Florida, is a celebration of authentic Jamaican jerk and includes a jerk cook-off competition, Jamaican cultural displays, and live entertainment. In recent years, jerk seasoning, which is a combination of allspice and scotch bonnet peppers, has become increasingly popular in the United States.

(continued from page 117)

children of Jamaican parents growing up in America struggle to find their own sense of belonging. In the face of being considered a "no-one," many young men choose to become someone by belonging to a gang with its strict codes of conduct and strong sense of identity. This sets a challenge for the Jamaican-American community and the wider American community to provide better alternatives to ghettoization.

IMMIGRATION AND BEING AN IMMIGRANT

Although since 1965 Jamaica has been one of the top sending countries, the number of Jamaicans arriving in North America is very small compared to other immigrant communities. In Canada, immigrants from the United Kingdom are by far the biggest group, with Italy and Hong Kong following. In the United States, Mexicans make up nearly 20 percent of the immigrants, with Jamaicans only accounting for about 1.5 percent. In many countries, immigration raises fears among the host population, sometimes out of proportion to the numbers. It is worth remembering that the vast majority of people living in North America were at one stage or other also immigrants.

That said, the experience of being an immigrant can also vary enormously. The prejudices faced by Irish, Italian, and Mexican immigrants to North America are different than those faced by Jamaicans. This is because the immigrants arrived carrying different histories and with different options available. Jamaicans often faced overt and covert racial prejudice based on their skin color rather than their identity as Jamaicans. Despite these experiences, many Jamaicans go on to achieve considerable success in public life and contribute to the social, cultural, and economic success of Canada and the United States. Evidence also shows that immigrant communities contribute far more to the host economies than they ever use or send back to relatives. However, this is not always a clear equation to draw, and Jamaican communities living overseas are often also seen as contributing to crime and violence.

WE LIKKLE BUT WE TALLAWAH!

Perhaps Jamaica's greatest achievement involves its musicians' contributions to popular culture, largely through the global music industry. Jamaica is a small country that, in cultural terms, has achieved a prominence far greater than its population of 2.7 million might suggest. Ever since Bob Marley became an international success, Jamaican styles and musical innovations have dramatically influenced the development of popular music. Reggae, rap, hip-hop, and dancehall are played globally, and few pop artists are immune to the influences first developed on Jamaican "lawns" and in dancehalls. As they say in Jamaican patois (the Jamaican creole language), *"we likkle but we tallawah,"* which means, "although we are a small country, we are great!" Like Jamaicans, Jamaican immigrants are small in number but have made a big impact on life in North America.

• Study Questions •

1. What history have you inherited?

2. Where did your ancestors come from and why did they move?

3. In your opinion, what is the most important factor influencing Jamaican immigration?

4. In your opinion, what are the biggest challenges facing the Jamaican-American community in the future?

5. What, in your opinion, has been the most important contribution of Jamaican immigrants to their chosen countries?

Chronology

A.D. 900 Taino Amerindians arrive in Jamaica.

1494 Christopher Columbus lands on the northern coast of Jamaica on May 6.

1510 First Spanish settlement is established on Jamaica.

1655 British take control of Jamaica.

1670 Britain signs treaty with Spain.

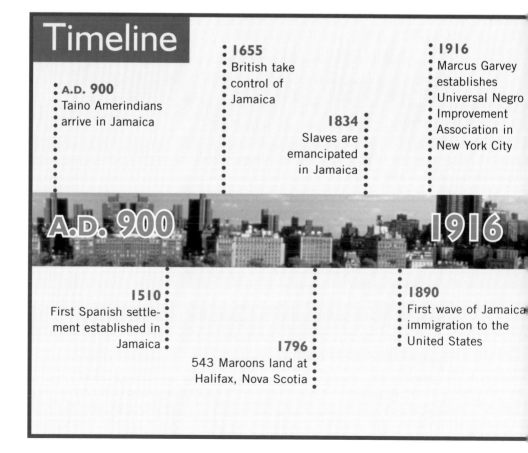

Timeline

A.D. 900
Taino Amerindians arrive in Jamaica

1510
First Spanish settlement established in Jamaica

1655
British take control of Jamaica

1834
Slaves are emancipated in Jamaica

1796
543 Maroons land at Halifax, Nova Scotia

1890
First wave of Jamaica immigration to the United States

1916
Marcus Garvey establishes Universal Negro Improvement Association in New York City

A.D. 900

1916

1700   Transatlantic slave trade increases.

1796   543 Maroons land in North America at Halifax, Nova Scotia, on July 22.

1831   Christmas Rebellion is led by Samuel Sharpe.

1834   Slaves are emancipated in Jamaica.

1845   First indentured laborers from India and China arrive in Jamaica.

1852   Robert Sutherland graduates from Queen's University.

1865   Morant Bay Rebellion occurs on October 11.

1890   The first wave of Jamaican immigration to the United States begins.

1916   Marcus Garvey establishes New York City

1962
Jamaica gains independence

1995
Sheila Jackson Lee elected to U.S. House of Representatives

1924
U.S. Immigration Act of 1924 passed

1988
Jamaican bobsled team competes at Winter Olympics

1924

2001

1965
United States passes Immigration and Naturalization Services Act

1952
United States passes McCarran-Walter Act

2001
Colin Powell becomes U.S. secretary of state

chapter of the Universal Negro Improvement Association (UNIA).

1922 Claude McKay publishes *Harlem Shadows*, which is among the early works of the Harlem Renaissance.

1924 U.S. Immigration Act of 1924 is passed; it restricts Jamaican immigration to the United States.

1936 Jamaica Progressive League of New York is established.

1938 Rebellion occurs at Frome Sugar Estate.

1952 United States passes McCarran-Walter Act, which restricts immigration from British Caribbean countries.

1956 Harry Belafonte's *Calypso* becomes the first LP to sell one million copies.

1962 Jamaica becomes independent on August 6; Canada passes the Immigration Regulations Act; Jamaican Canadian Association formed.

1965 United States passes the Immigration and Naturalization Services Act.

1967 Canada passes Immigration Act of 1967.

1968 Lincoln Alexander is elected to the House of Commons.

1972 Dr. Rosemary Brown is elected to the provincial legislature of British Columbia.

1977 West Indian Jets Soccer Club represents Illinois in the United States Cup.

1988 Jamaican bobsled team competes in the Calgary Winter Olympics.

1991 Una Clarke becomes first Jamaican and Caribbean city council member in New York City.

1995 Sheila Jackson Lee is elected to the U.S. House of Representatives.

1996   Donovan Bailey wins an Olympic gold medal at the Summer Olympics.

1997   Rachel Manley wins the Governor General's Literary Award for her book *Drumblair*.

1999   Bob Marley's *Exodus* is named album of the century by *Time* magazine.

2001   General Colin Powell becomes the U.S. secretary of state; U.S. PATRIOT Act is passed.

2002   Canada passes Immigrant and Refugee Protection Act.

2003   Alvin Curling is named speaker of the legislature in Canada.

2004   Caribefest takes place in Miami.

Notes

Chapter 3

1. *The Register,* Thursday, August 7, 1902. Available online at *http://www.rootsweb.com/~canbrnep/jammaroon.htm.*
2. The first bananas were imported to the United States in 1870, and just 28 years later, Americans were consuming more than 16 million bunches a year.
3. Philip Kasinitz, *Caribbean New York: Black Immigrants and the Politics of Race* (Ithaca and London: Cornell University Press, 1992).

Chapter 4

4. Except Puerto Ricans, who have a special status in the United States.
5. Nancy Foner, *In a New Land: A Comparative View of Immigration* (New York: New York University Press, 2005).
6. Ceri Peach, *West Indian Migration to Britain* (London: Oxford University Press, 1968), and Foner, *In a New Land.*
7. Peach, *West Indian Migration to Britain.*
8. Quote from interview with coauthor (Horst, 2004).

Chapter 5

9. Elizabeth Thomas-Hope, "Globalization and the Development of a Caribbean Migration Culture," In *Caribbean Migration* by M. Chamberlain (London: Routledge, 1998) 188–202.
10. *The Jamaica Gleaner* (Monday, November 14, 2005).

Chapter 6

11. Kasinitz, *Caribbean New York.*
12. Frances Henry, *The Caribbean Diaspora in Toronto: Learning to Live With Racism* (Toronto, Buffalo, and London: University of Toronto Press), 1994.
13. Ibid.
14. Milton Vickerman, *Crosscurrents: West Indian Immigrants and Race* (New York and Oxford: Oxford University Press), 1999.

Chapter 7

15. Foner, *In a New Land: A Comparative View of Immigration*
16. Quote from interview with coauthor (Horst, 2004).
17. Heather A. Horst and Daniel Miller, *The Cell Phone: An Anthropology of Communication*

(Oxford and New York: Berg
Press, 2006).

Chapter 9

18. 6th Annual Jamerican Film
and Music Festival. Available online at *http://www.jameri-canfilmfestival.com/template.
php?page=text/festival_history.
html.*

Glossary

Africville A small community adjacent to Halifax, Nova Scotia, entirely populated by black families from a wide variety of origins. The community and its dwellings were ordered destroyed, and residents evicted during the late 1960s.

assimilation A cultural policy in countries such as the United States that encourages immigrants and minorities to "melt" into society, or to adapt to the customs and practices of their new or dominant society.

Bogle, Paul (1820?–1865) A Baptist deacon who was a peaceful man, but ended up leading the Morant Bay Rebellion in 1865. He is considered one of the heroes of Jamaica.

Bustamante, Alexander (1884–1977) A Jamaican politician and labor leader who became a prominent figure in the struggle against colonial rule particularly through labor strikes. He was the founder of the Jamaica Labour Party and received the instruments of independence from the queen.

CARICOM An acronym for the Caribbean Community, established in 1973 to coordinate common policies among the member states, including a single Caribbean market, legal system, and passport agreements. As of 2006, CARICOM consisted of the following members: Antigua and Barbuda, Bahamas, Barbados, Belize, Dominica, Grenada, Guyana, Haiti, Jamaica, Montserrat, Saint Kitts and Nevis, Saint Lucia, Saint Vincent and the Grenadines, Suriname and Trinidad, and Tobago.

child-shifting When families send their children to live temporarily with friends and neighbors, often because the parents believe that the alternative homes will be a better place for their children.

Commonwealth Sometimes called the Commonwealth of Nations, the group is made up of 53 former members and colonies of the British Empire, including the United Kingdom, Jamaica, India, Australia, Canada, South Africa, and Singapore.

Cudjoe   The Maroon leader responsible for the compromise with the British in 1740. He was a short, almost dwarflike man who for years fought skillfully and bravely to maintain his people's independence.

deportation   The act of sending an individual out of a country. Although all governments can force individuals to leave, individuals are usually deported only when they commit a crime.

Garvey, Marcus (1887–1940)   A publisher, journalist, entrepreneur, and crusader for black nationalism. He founded the Universal Negro Improvement Association and strongly supported the "back to Africa" movement.

Gold Coast   The area in the Horn of Africa, where the vast majority of slaves were taken from. The area is roughly the same as modern Ghana.

Gordon, George William (1820–1865)   The son of a planter and a slave who was a critic of the colonial government. He established the Native Baptist Church where Paul Bogle was deacon. After the Morant Bay Rebellion, he was sentenced to death. His execution and the brutality of the suppression became notorious in Britain.

indentured labor   Laborers who came from India whose passage was paid for in return for work. The idea was they would work to pay off the costs of transportation. In reality, the system was carefully set up to ensure they never achieved this.

Jamaica Labour Party (JLP)   Founded in 1943 by Alexander Bustamante as the political wing of the Bustamante Industrial Trade Union. It ruled from independence in 1962 to 1972 and from 1980 to 1989.

Jamaican Assembly   The governing body of Jamaica, which, during most of the slave trade period, managed affairs to favor plantation owners. Representatives on the assembly were overwhelmingly planters.

Manley, Norman (1893–1969)   Jamaican political leader and one of Jamaica's leading lawyers in the 1920s. He was an advocate of universal suffrage and founder of the left-wing People's National Party (PNP).

Maroons   Escaped slaves who lived in independent communities in the mountainous interior of Jamaica. The British were unable to defeat them, despite major attempts in the 1730s and

1790s. Under treaties signed with the colonial government, the Maroons captured and returned escaped plantation slaves.

McKay, Claude (1889–1948)   Jamaican writer and poet who played an important part in the Harlem Renaissance with his book of poetry, *Harlem Shadows* (1922). *Home to Harlem* (1928) was a bestseller that won the Harmon Gold Award for Literature.

multiculturalism   A cultural policy adopted by countries such as Canada to help understand and manage people of different cultures. In contrast to assimilation, where cultural differences are downplayed for the common good, multiculturalism encourages the expression of cultural difference as long as people agree to live together as one nation.

partners   A popular form of savings in Jamaica (and other Caribbean countries). It is a system for groups of people who know each other and is often the only way for poor people in Jamaica to save.

People's National Party (PNP)   Founded by Norman Manley in 1938, it is the oldest political party in the Anglophone Caribbean. The PNP held a majority in the Jamaican Parliament from 1972 to 1980, and, from 1989 to date. In 2006, Portia Simpson Miller, the first female prime minister, led the party to victory.

remittances   The transfer of money by foreign workers to their home country. This often occurs through couriers and banking services such as Money Gram, Western Union, and other special agencies.

saltfish   Fish preserved in salt. Once washed, the fish is cooked and often served with Ackee—a Jamaican fruit that looks and tastes like scrambled egg.

Sharpe, Sam "Daddy" (1801–1832)   A slave throughout his life, Sharpe became well-educated and known as a preacher and leader. He organized a peaceful strike across many parts of Jamaica when he thought emancipation had already been declared. A rebellion occurred in 1831 and Sharpe was blamed and hanged in 1832.

Taino   The indigenous Amerindian inhabitants of Jamaica prior to European contact. Their language is thought to have been a form of Arawak.

transnationalism   The maintenance of connections between two different countries or members of two different countries. For Jamaican Americans, transnationalism is aided by relatively inexpensive telephone service, Internet connections, plane flights, and other forms of movement and communication among Jamaicans in North America and around the world.

West Indians   People from one of the 28 territories in and around the Caribbean Sea, including Jamaica, the Bahamas, Barbados, the Cayman Islands, Grenada, Guyana, Saint Lucia, Trinidad and Tobago (among others). Today, the area has a regional university, the University of the West Indies, with campuses in Barbados, Jamaica, Trinidad and Tobago, and the Bahamas.

Bibliography

Chamberlain, Mary, ed. *Caribbean Migration: Globalised Identities.* New York: Routledge, 1999.

Chevannes, Barry. *Rastafari: Roots and Ideology.* Syracuse, N.Y.: Syracuse University Press, 1994.

Foner, Nancy. *In a New Land: A Comparative View of Immigration.* New York: New York University Press, 2005.

——. "Towards a Comparative Perspective on Caribbean Migration." In *Caribbean Migration: Globalized Identities,* edited by M. Chamberlain. London: Routledge, 1998, pp. 47–62.

——. "What's New About Transnationalism? New York Immigrants Today and at the Turn of the Century." *Diaspora* vol. 6, no. 3 (1997): 355–375.

——. *Islands in the City: West Indian Migration to New York.* Berkeley and Los Angeles: University of California Press, 2001.

Henke, Holger. *The West Indian Americans.* Westport, Conn.: Greenwood Press, 2001.

Henry, Frances. *The Caribbean Diaspora in Toronto: Learning to Live With Racism.* Toronto, Buffalo, and London: University of Toronto Press, 1994.

——. "Caribbean Migration to Canada: Prejudice and Opportunity." In *The Caribbean Exodus* by B.B. Levine. New York: Praeger Press, 1987, pp. 214–224.

——. and Dwaine Plaza, eds. *Returning to the Source.* Kingston, Jamaica: University of the West Indies Press, 2006.

Hintzen, Percy C. *West Indian in the West: Self-Representation in an Immigrant Community.* New York: New York University Press, 2001.

Horst, Heather A., and Daniel Miller. *The Cell Phone: An Anthropology of Communication.* Oxford and New York: Berg Press, 2006.

Kasinitz, Philip. *Caribbean New York: Black Immigrants and the Politics of Race.* Ithaca and London: Cornell University Press, 1992.

Model, Suzanne, Gene Fisher, and Roxane Silberman. "Black Caribbeans in Comparative Perspective." *Journal of Ethnic and Migration Studies* vol. 25, no. 2 (1999): pp. 187–212.

Momsen, Janet H. "Gender Selectivity in Caribbean Migration." In *Gender and Migration in Developing Countries* by S. Chant. London: Bellhaven Press, 1992, pp. 73–90.

Olwig, Karen Fog. "A 'Respectable' Livelihood: Mobility and Identity in a Caribbean Family." In *Work and Migration: Life and Livelihoods in a Globalizing World* by N. N. Sorensen and K. F. Olwig. London and New York: Routledge, 2002, pp. 85–105.

Peach, Ceri. *West Indian Migration to Britain: A Social Geography.* London: Oxford University Press, 1968.

Pessar, Patricia R., ed. *Caribbean Circuits: New Directions in the Study of Caribbean Migration.* Staten Island, N.Y.: Center for Migration Studies, 1997.

Soto, Isa M. "West Indian Child Fostering: Its Role in Migrant Exchanges." In *Caribbean Life in New York* by C. Sutton and E. M. Chaney. New York: Center for Migration Studies, 1987, pp. 121–137.

Sutton, Constance, and Elsa M. Chaney, eds. *Caribbean Life in New York City: Sociocultural Dimensions.* New York: Center for Migration Studies of New York, 1987.

Thomas-Hope, Elizabeth. "Globalization and the Development of a Caribbean Migration Culture." In *Caribbean Migration* by M. Chamberlain. London: Routledge, 1998, pp. 188–202.

Vickerman, Milton. *Crosscurrents: West Indian Immigrants and Race.* New York and Oxford: Oxford University Press, 1999.

Further Reading

Manley, Rachel. *Drumblair: Memories of a Jamaican Childhood.* Kingston, Jamaica: Ian Randle Publishers, 1996.

——. *In My Father's Shade.* London: Black Amber Books, 2004.

Sherlock, Philip, and Hazel Bennett. *The Story of the Jamaican People.* Kingston, Jamaica: Ian Randle Publishers, 1998.

White, Timothy. *To Catch a Fire: The Life of Bob Marley.* New York: Henry Holt, 1998.

NOVELS

Cliff, Michelle. *Free Enterprise: A Novel of Mary Ellen Pleasant.* San Francisco: City Lights Publishers, 2004.

——. *No Telephone to Heaven.* New York: Plume Books, 1996.

Levy, Andrea. *Never Far From Nowhere.* London: Headline Review Press (Hodder Headline), 1996.

——. *Small Island.* New York: Picador Press (St. Martin's Press), 2004.

Smith, Zadie. *On Beauty.* New York: Penguin Press, 2005.

——. *White Teeth.* New York: Vintage Books, 2001.

WEB SITES

"Religion by Location,"Adherents.com
http://www.adherents.com/adhloc/Wh_161.html

The American Immigration Homepage
 http://www.bergen.org/AAST/Projects/Immigration/

U.S. Census Information
http://www.census.gov/population/cen2000/stp-159/stp159-jamaica.pdf.

"Geography and History of Jamaica," The Gleaner
http://www.discoverjamaica.com/gleaner/discover/geography

"Claude McKay's Life," Modern American Poetry
http://www.english.uiuc.edu/maps/poets/m_r/mckay/life.htm

U.S. Census Bureau
http://factfinder.census.gov/home/saff/main.html?_lang=en.

Information on Marcus Garvey
http://homeworkhelp.aol.com/printcanvas/_a/who-was-marcus-garvey/.

"The Story of Spanish Town," The Gleaner
http://www.jamaica-gleaner.com/pages/history/story0049.htm

"History of Jamaica," Government of Jamaica
http://www.jis.gov.jm/gov_ja/history.asp

"National Heroes," The Jamaican Information Service
http://www.jis.gov.jm/special_sections/Heroes/Heroes1.htm.

"A Message From the Minister of Education," Jamaica Ministry of
     Education, Youth, and Culture, National Heroes of Jamaica
http://www.kasnet.com/heroesofjamaica/start/

Rastafari Ring
http://members.aol.com/rasjoshi/rastafariring.htm.

"The Jamaican Maroons," The Register Newspaper of the Town of
     Berwick, Kings County, Nova Scotia, First Published in 1891
http://www.rootsweb.com/~canbrnep/jammaroon.htm.

"Exhibition: Claude McKay," Harlem 1900–1940, Schomberg Cent-
     er for Research in Black Culture
http://www.si.umich.edu/CHICO/Harlem/text/mckay.html

"The Harlem Exhibit: Marcus Mosiah Garvey," The Schomburg
     Center for Research in Black Culture
http://www.si.umich.edu/CHICO/Harlem/text/garvey.html

"Statistics Canada," Canada's National Statistical Agency
http://www40.statcan.ca/l01/cst01/demo26a.htm

The Declaration of Rights of the Negro People of the World and
     The Universal Ethiopian Anthem Available online
http://www.unia-acl.org/archieve/decalre.htm.

"UNIA History," UNIA-ACL
http://www.unia-acl.org/info/historic.htm.

Picture Credits

Index

About the Contributors

Series Editor **Robert D. Johnston** is associate professor and director of the Teaching of History Program in the Department of History at the University of Illinois at Chicago. He is the author of *The Making of America: The History of the United States from 1492 to the Present*, a middle-school textbook that received a *School Library Journal* Best Book of the Year Award. He is currently working on a history of vaccine controversies in American history, to be published by Oxford University Press.

Heather A. Horst is a postdoctoral scholar at the Institute for the Study of Social Change, University of California, Berkeley. She worked as a teaching assistant at a rural primary school in Jamaica and studied Jamaican migration, return migration, and transnationalism. Her most recent work, *The Cell Phone: An Anthropology of Communication* (with Daniel Miller, Berg Press), focuses upon the integration of new communication technologies in Jamaica and the implications of these technologies for development as well as communication between Jamaicans at home and abroad.

Andrew Garner is honorary research associate at Oxford Brookes University in the United Kingdom. His postdoctoral research on environmental conflicts in a marine park in Jamaica entailed spending a year with Jamaican fishermen learning about their lives and, in the process, becoming reasonably good at fishing. His publications include an edited journal edition of *Worldviews* (10:2 2006) on the meaning of water, and "Moral meeting places in an uncivil society: local stakeholders and environmental protection in Jamaica" in *Vision and Execution in Environmental Conservation: Virtualism, Governance and Practice* edited by James Carrier and Paige West. He is interested in applying anthropological knowledge to real-world problems and is a committee member of the UK *Association of Social Anthropology*.